Social

How to Surv

LIBRARY OF CONGRESS CATALOGING IN PUBLICATION
DATA
Martin, Mozelle
Social Media Monsters: How to Survive Creeps with Keyboards
Pages 273
Does Not Include Index
Printed in the United States of America
ISBN 978-1-312-41635-2

Cover design by Grafiz_Designs on Fiverr.com

Table of Contents

Inventory of YouTube Channels I Follow:

Dedication

To all the adult professionals who have confronted the darkest corners of the digital world, where cruelty and malice thrive, your strength and resilience serve as an inspiration to everyone. Despite the vicious attacks on your character, you have triumphed over the storm, refusing to let cyber-hatred define you.

This dedication honors your unwavering determination, spirit, and commitment to your chosen path. You have faced the worst aspects of humanity, yet your light continues to shine, guiding you along a compassionate and professional journey.

May this book act as a shield against the continued and relentless storm of cyber-hatred, equipping you with knowledge, insights, and strategies. May it empower you and remind you that you are not alone in this fight. This dedication solemnly vows to champion your cause, raise awareness, and cultivate a world where respect, empathy, and kindness prevail.

This book is dedicated to you - *the survivors, the warriors, the relentless professionals* - who refuse to be silenced. Your voices matter, your stories matter, and together, we can stand tall and united against the vicious targeting that seeks to undermine our collective well-being.

With utmost respect and unwavering support,

Mozelle

Thoughts & Insights:

Supporting the Mission: Key Strategies

Will you pleasc help support my mission?

➢ **Purchase this book**: By obtaining a copy of this book, you directly contribute to its overall success and help raise public awareness. It also makes a thoughtful gift for family, friends, and coworkers who are advocates for change and / or online content creators.

➢ **Leave reviews**: Share your positive feedback by leaving reviews on online bookstores, social media platforms, or personal blogs. These reviews generate excitement and attract new readers. Your honest and thoughtful reviews play a significant role in making this book an important victim advocate tool.

➢ **Recommend this book**: Spread the word about this book among your social circles, including friends, family, book clubs, and online communities. Word-of-mouth recommendations are powerful in increasing exposure and reaching a wider audience.

➢ **Engage on social media**: Take a photo of yourself with the book and tag me! You can also use the optional hashtags mentioned in the book. Active participation on social media helps create visibility and encourage others to join in the conversation.

➢ **Request the book at local bookstores and libraries**: Visit your local bookstore or library and request they carry a few copies of this book by giving them the ISBN. This initiative helps others in your community gain insights in dealing with online harassment. Additionally, you can purchase a few copies and directly donate them to the library.

Remember, every act helps make a meaningful difference for others and I am grateful for the support of dedicated readers like you.

Thoughts & Insights:

What to Expect

This captivating book takes readers on a journey into the intricate world of cyber-hatred. It begins with a detailed section that provides a clear understanding of key concepts and terminology.

In the introduction, I share a deeply personal and relatable account of my own experience with cyber-hatred, explaining the motivation behind writing this book.

The book explores the multifaceted aspects of cyber-hatred, offering a comprehensive understanding of the behavioral and psychological dimensions displayed by online perpetrators, commonly referred to as "haters," "monsters," and "creeps." These terms are used in alignment with the book's title and are not intended as personal insults. Allow me to briefly elucidate the significance behind the title. The term "monsters" is employed because these individuals launch unexpected attacks for unknown reasons, reminiscent of the behavior of monsters. Just as we were afraid of monsters lurking under our beds or in dark closets during our childhood, cyber-hatred can instill a similar sense of fear.

Additionally, the term "creeps" is used to depict how these individuals stealthily infiltrate your life, operating discreetly in the background, often assuming false identities and profile pictures. It is important to acknowledge that these "monsters" and "creeps" primarily engage in such behavior to spread "hatred" throughout your online experiences.

Keeping that in mind, the aim of this book is to deepen readers' comprehension of the subject matter by introducing the prevalent types of *haters, monsters,* and *creeps* encountered in the digital realm. It seeks to shed light on their potentially sinister motives, offering valuable insights into their behavior.

Recognizing that knowledge is power, the book reveals the common tactics employed by "haters," "monsters," and "creeps." It delves into the strategies used to demean, intimidate, and harass their victims, equipping readers with crucial information for self-defense and mitigation.

To strengthen my arguments, I incorporate brief case studies of other victims alongside my personal story. These additional individuals represent just a small sampling of those who have faced similar hardships. I also present a wealth of evidence gathered by myself and my legal team, which substantiates my own experience and emphasizes its implications across society.

The book also offers valuable self-help resources for victims to navigate the challenges they face.

Furthermore, it includes a comprehensive reference list, serving as a valuable starting point for readers interested in conducting independent research on this growing problem.

Moreover, sarcastic graphics complement the content, adding humor to alleviate challenging situations.

Lastly, the book includes pages for note-taking in the "thoughts & insights" section, an area for readers to add their favorite external and empowering quotes, and space to write the names of those who would benefit from having a copy of this book in their collection, making it suitable as a gift-giving reference.

"Because spreading love and kindness is so mainstream, let's all be cyber-haters!"

(sarcasm fully intended)

Thoughts & Insights:

A-Z List of Terms

This book includes a comprehensive list of terms that will greatly aid in understanding its content. If you already possess a solid understanding of technology, feel free to skip this section.

- **Aggressor**: person or group responsible for initiating cyberbullying or other online tactics; also considered cyberbully (ies).
- **Anonymous Threats**: threatening or intimidating messages sent to the target or victim anonymously.
- **Avatar**: a digital representation of oneself used in online forums, social media, and gaming platforms, often similar to a cartoon.
- **Bad actors**: used for many years in various fields including performing arts, politics, and technology. This term refers to individuals or groups who engage in malicious activities, such as hacking, identity theft, or spreading malware. Originating in the cybersecurity industry, this term has become a popular way to describe individuals or groups who engage in harmful behavior, including for the purpose of cyberbullying and cyber-drama. *Ironically, one of my haters has publicly stated repeatedly that he coined that term. No, he didn't and yes, I have proof.*
- **Baiting**: a tactic used by cyber-haters to deliberately provoke or manipulate their victims into reacting impulsively. It involves intentionally posting provocative, offensive, or controversial content with the goal to create discord, provoke conflict, or entertain oneself at the expense of their victims.
- **Block**: preventing someone from contacting you or viewing your online content.
- **Bullycide**: used to describe victims who ended their life because of being cyberattacked.

- **Bystander**: a person who witnesses cyberbullying but does not intervene or report it. While being an online bystander is not a criminal offense in and of itself, there are situations where an online bystander could potentially be charged with a crime. For example, if an online bystander witnesses a crime being committed and fails to report it, they could be charged with 'accessory after the fact,' 'obstruction of justice,' or similar crimes.
- **Cancel culture**: is the practice of publicly shaming, boycotting, or otherwise ostracizing individuals or groups who have expressed opinions or behaviors that are considered socially unacceptable or offensive. This often occurs in politics, free speech, history, culture, and social media.
- **Catfishing**: a form of cyberbullying that involves creating a fake identity or online persona to deceive or manipulate someone.
- **Content creator**: someone who makes and shares different types of content on the internet, like videos, articles, social media posts, podcasts, and more. They can work alone or with a team and cover lots of topics, like entertainment, education, news, and opinions. Content creators use online platforms and tools, such as YouTube, Instagram, TikTok, blogs, and websites and often use special cameras, microphones, and software. Content creation is a popular way to express opinions, share hobbies and expertise, and it also encourages worldwide collaboration. Many content creators have big followings and turn their hobby into a full-time job.
- **Cyber bullying prevention**: efforts to prevent cyber bullying and online harassment, including education, awareness-raising campaigns, and policies and guidelines for safe and responsible online behavior.
- **Cyber bullying**: such as posting, sharing, or sending harmful, false, or mean content about someone with

the intent of causing harm, embarrassment, or humiliation. This behavior often breaks the law.

- **Cyber defense**: the practice of protecting against and responding to cyber-attacks, including network security, incident response planning, and risk management.
- **Cyber exploitation**: using digital technology to exploit or harm others through theft or manipulation of personal data or intellectual property.
- **Cyber fraud:** fraudulent activities carried out online, such as identity theft, phishing scams, or fake investment schemes.
- **Cyber governance**: set of policies and procedures to guide the use of digital technology and data, including security, privacy, and compliance.
- **Cyber harm**: any negative consequences caused by malicious online actions. This includes damage, loss, or injury resulting from cyberbullying, cyberstalking, cyber harassment, or any other type of online abuse. The harm can be direct, like emotional distress, financial loss, or damage to one's reputation. It can also be indirect, like experiencing secondary trauma by witnessing online abuse directed at others. With the increase in technology for business, cyber harm is becoming a growing concern.
- **Cyber insurance policy**: mostly for businesses, this provides coverage against losses or damages resulting from cyber-attacks or data breaches.
- **Cyber security awareness**: efforts to promote awareness and understanding of cyber risks and best practices through training, education, and outreach.
- **Cyber vigilante**: someone who takes the law into their own hands to pursue justice against cyber criminals or other online wrongdoers.
- **Cyber violence**: using digital technology to perpetrate violence or harm, including threats, and hate speech.

- **Cyber warfare**: using technology to conduct military operations such as hacking, spying, and propaganda campaigns.
- **Cybercrime**: criminal activities committed using technology such as hacking, financial fraud, identity theft, and often, this crosses over into cyberbullying.
- **Cyber-drama**: Online conflicts and controversies that frequently occur when personal or sensitive information is exposed or shared on social platforms. These conflicts can involve public arguments, online harassment, and cyberbullying. People or groups often take sides and engage in intense debates or discussions, which can escalate and become hostile or threatening. While some conflicts may be entertaining, there is a delicate boundary between those that are harmless and those that have severe consequences, such as reputation damage, emotional harm, or even legal and disciplinary actions. Many content creators engage in such conflicts for the purpose of gaining likes, clicks, and financial benefits.
- **Cyber-ethics**: principles and values that guide ethical behavior and decision-making in the online environment including interactions with others while respecting their privacy, transparency, honesty, opinions, lifestyles, etc.
- **Cyber-harassment**: using digital technology to harass, intimidate, or threaten others, including through abusive or derogatory messages, audio clips, videos, posts, or images.
- **Cyber-hate**: form of cyberbullying that involves spreading hateful, biased, and abusive messages directed toward an individual or group of people using digital technology.
- **Cyber-hygiene**: maintaining good cyber habits and behaviors, including strong passwords, updated software, and avoiding unknown links and downloads.

- **Cyber-intelligence**: collecting, analyzing, and interpreting data from digital sources to identify and prevent cyberthreats, such as hacking, cyberterrorism, and many others listed in this section.
- **Cyber-libel**: publicly stating untrue and damaging claims about someone else on the internet. This includes message or bulletin boards, blogs, chat rooms, websites, social media, articles, and more.
- **Cyber-mobbing**: a form of cyberbullying where a group of people gang up on an individual to attack, humiliate, or exclude them (social ostracizing is the term often used). I call them the "monster mob" or "monster club members."
- **Cyber-predator**: an individual who uses technology to target and groom vulnerable individuals, often children, for sexual exploitation and other abuse.
- **Cyber-resilience**: the ability to prepare for, withstand, and recover (survive) cyber-attacks and other digital disruptions. This could include through contingency planning, redundancy, backup systems, support groups, and similar for both the system itself and individuals who are targeted victims. The resource section should help you with this.
- **Cybersecurity breach**: unauthorized intrusion or attack on a computer system or network that results in theft, damage, or other intentional acts of harm.
- **Cyber-shaming**: publicly shaming someone online for their behavior, career, or anything else the individual or group does not agree with as a way to make them quit or coerce them into compliance. This is often referred to as social ostracizing or social consequences.
- **Cyber-slander (defamation)**: keep in mind that this is only illegal in states where defamation is illegal. Closely related to cyber-libel, perpetrators claim "First Amendment" rights under "freedom of speech" even though they can still be sued for defamation. Slander or defamation is when someone makes false

statements but claims they are fact. The results of their lies cause mental, physical, spiritual, or financial harm. This is one of the most common cybercrimes due to the ease of finding personal information online. Many attorneys will not accept these cases, but more on this later in this book.

- **Cyber-stalking**: repeated following, tracking, or monitoring someone's online activity without their consent, often with the intention of causing harm or intimidation. In line with this are the cyberstalking laws that prohibit and punish those engaged in harassment and abuse.

- **Cyber-terrorism**: using technology to intimidate, harm, or disrupt a country's political or social systems through hacking critical infrastructures.

- **Cyber-trickery**: initially used to identify spear-phishing or social engineering to gain financial benefits. It has since been categorized as a mode of cyberbullying similar to outing. The difference being that the trick occurs when the perpetrator strategically deceives the victim.

- **Deepfake**: a manipulated video or audio recording that uses artificial intelligence (A.I.) to create realistic but false content, often for malicious purposes such as spreading disinformation, misinformation, and cyberbullying.

- **Denigration**: spreading false and harmful information about someone online.

- **Digital citizenship**: responsible use of technology and online platforms, including respecting the privacy, opinions, careers, and lifestyles of others, thereby promoting cyber-respect

- **Digital footprint**: trail of digital information that people leave behind when they use the internet, social media, or other digital devices.

- **Digital literacy**: ability to effectively and responsibly use technology and online platforms for critical thinking, media fluency, and online safety.
- **Dirty Deleting**: refers to the act of an individual deleting or hiding offensive or harmful comments or messages previously posted after realizing the negative impact they had or may have. This behavior can be seen as an attempt to evade responsibility and avoid potential consequences for their actions. Dirty deleting in cyberbullying not only attempts to erase evidence of the harmful behavior but also undermines the victim's ability to collect evidence or seek support, making it more difficult to address the issue. *However, more on this later; it is not always what it seems.*
- **Disinformation**: deliberately spreading false or misleading information with the intention of deceiving or manipulating people. Often spread by individuals, organizations, or governments with a specific agenda or motive to sway public opinion, discredit opponents, or create confusion. It is *always* intentionally untrue or misleading.
- **Doxing (Doxxing)**: is the act of publishing someone's personal or private information online. This can include their home address, phone number, medical information, criminal history, family member's private information, email addresses, and more to harass or intimidate them.
- **Encryption**: converting data into a secret code or cipher to protect it from unauthorized access or theft.
- **Exclusion**: excluding someone from an online community is often a form of cyberbullying. This is an intentional act of leaving someone out of online conversations or activities.
- **Fake profile**: creating a social media or online profile under false pretenses to harass or deceive others.

- **Firewall**: network security system that monitors and controls incoming and outgoing traffic based on predetermined security rules and codes.
- **Flaming**: sending angry or aggressive messages online, often in response to a disagreement or conflict. It is a form of cyberbullying that involves using aggressive or inflammatory language to attack someone online.
- **Flying monkeys**: individuals who assist or support the primary cyber-hater in targeting and harassing a victim. They are typically friends, followers, or acquaintances of the main instigator who are willing to join in to amplify the attacks or spread rumors about the victim. They can significantly escalate the impact and reach of the cyberhatred. This is also referred to as cyber mob, cyber army, or gang-stalking (below).
- **Fraping**: when a third party makes a change to your social networking account without your awareness or consent. For example, if a bully uses your Facebook account to post inappropriate content under your name.
- **Gang-stalking (organized)**: considered a severe form of harassment, involving multiple users working together with malicious intent to bring significant harm to their target's life. The ultimate goal is to cause their victim to experience extreme mental distress, jail or hospital visits, chronic mental, emotional, or physical suffering, financial loss, homelessness, or even suicide through coordinated efforts. Efforts include making false accusations, starting rumors, inciting bogus investigations, setting up traps, framing the victim, using intimidation and threats (overt and covert), engaging in vandalism, theft, sabotage, torture, humiliation, emotional terrorism, and more. This collective action is often led by a central figure, such as a popular YouTube creator, along with their loyal subscribers who actively and knowingly participate in

the organized and systematic harassment of the victim.

- **Gaslighting**: manipulating someone into questioning their own sanity or reality.
- **Griefing**: intentionally disrupting or causing chaos in an online game or community.
- **Grifter**: a manipulative individual who deceives others and gains their trust for personal gain. They pretend to be an expert in a specific area, but their intentions are not genuine. Instead, they exploit their followers by scamming or defrauding them, often by selling fake products, services, or investment opportunities. They are skilled at being convincing and persuasive, employing tactics like instilling fear, offering flattery, and making emotional appeals to establish trust. They may also employ tactics such as creating fake reviews, testimonials, and endorsements to give the impression of credibility and authenticity.
- **Hacking**: gaining unauthorized access to a computer system or network, devices, and even online profiles and accounts for the purpose of stealing data or causing malicious harm.
- **Harassment**: repeatedly sending offensive, threatening, or unwanted messages to someone online as a way to annoy, intimidate, or harm someone publicly.
- **Hate speech**: speech or language that promotes hatred, discrimination, or violence against a particular group of people based on their race, ethnicity, religion, gender, sexual orientation, and similar.
- **Hater-creators**: someone who creates content for the purpose of conducting cyber-hatred.
- **Impersonation**: creating fake social media accounts or email addresses while pretending to be someone else in order to deceive or harm others. This could also include hacking into someone's account or cloning their account.

- **IRL**: means "in real life" and is used to differentiate between online and in-person interactions.
- **Jokes**: Jokes that may appear humorous, but may be perceived as hurtful or offensive by the recipient. This is often referred to as "roasting".
- **Like-farming**: a cyber scam where one creates a post that appeals to people's emotions or interests to gain likes and shares. This is in line with cyber-drama.
- **Malware**: software designed to harm or damage computer networks or devices.
- **Masquerading**: pretending to be someone else online to deceive or harm others.
- **Misinformation**: inaccurate or false information *not* necessarily spread with malicious intent. Often this is a result of misunderstanding or misinterpretation. This can spread quickly on social media and other online platforms, often leading to confusion and uncertainty.
- **NSFW**: *"not safe for work"* and is almost always a pornographic or other content intended for adults only.
- **Negativity**: comments or messages intended to hurt, insult, or humiliate someone.
- **Netiquette**: rules of behavior that govern online communication and interactions. This is in line with being an upstander and good digital citizen.
- **Online identity**: the way people present themselves online, including their profiles, posts, and interactions.
- **Online privacy**: the right to control and protect one's own personal information and data online through privacy settings, encryption, and other security measures.
- **Online safety**: protecting oneself and others from online threats and harm, including through digital literacy, cybersecurity, and positive online behaviors.
- **Outing**: similar to doxing, the perpetrator shares secrets or private information online and this person is usually someone the victim knows.

- **Phishing**: using fraudulent emails or websites to obtain sensitive information, such as credit card info and passwords by tricking individuals.
- **Privacy**: the right to control who has access to your private information and its use.
- **Profile**: online representation of a person or organization for public view.
- **Puppet (Sock) accounts**: fake accounts that individuals create on social media platforms, online forums, or other websites. The purpose of these accounts is to conceal the person's true identity or deceive others into thinking they are someone else. Commonly used to manipulate online discussions, engage in harassment or bullying, spread false information or propaganda, or artificially boost the popularity of individuals or brands, they often have fake names, profile pictures, and personal details. They can be operated by one person or a group. These accounts violate terms of service on most online platforms and can lead to account suspension or termination.
- **Queerphobia**: discriminatory behavior towards people who identify as LGBTQ+ often manifested through online hate speech, cyberbullying, or harassment.
- **Ransomware**: malware that encrypts a victim's files or data and demands a ransom payment in exchange for restoring access to their own files.
- **Receipts**: sharing evidence or proof to back up a claim or accusation such as screenshots, photos, videos, etc. so prove the individual is telling the truth.
- **Revenge porn**: sharing sexually explicit images or videos of someone without their consent, often as a form of revenge, retaliation, or humiliation.
- **Rumors**: spreading false, malicious, or unverified information online with a goal of humiliation, or harassment.

- **Selfie**: self-portrait photograph in which the camera or phone is held at arm's length. Shared on social media platforms, they have become a popular form of self-expression and self-promotion. Although widespread in the early 2010s with the rise of smartphones, self-portraits have been common for centuries.
- **Sexting**: sending sexually explicit messages or images through digital technology. *This makes me question where self-respect went.*
- **Sextortion**: threatening to release intimate photos or videos of someone unless they comply with certain demands.
- **Slander**: false statement made orally that harms a person's reputation.
- **Social engineering**: manipulating people into revealing sensitive information or performing actions that lead to breaches or other forms of technological harm.
- **Social media addiction**: excessive and unhealthy reliance on social media and other technology, often leading to negative mental health symptoms and problems in personal and professional relationships.
- **Social media monitoring**: monitoring and analyzing online activity for the purpose of identifying and responding to online threats and attacks.
- **Social media**: websites that allow users to create and share content, connect with others, and participate in online communities.
- **Spoofing**: falsifying digital information to deceive or harm others, often by sending emails or messages that appear to be from a trusted source.
- **Swatting**: the act of making a false emergency report or hoax to law enforcement agencies, typically involving a claim of a serious threat or crime taking place at a specific location. The intention behind swatting is to provoke a response from highly trained

and heavily armed police teams, who are dispatched to the targeted location. Swatting incidents often involve a deliberate effort to deceive emergency services and cause a large-scale response, putting innocent individuals in danger and wasting valuable resources. The term "swatting" derives from the involvement of SWAT teams in responding to these false reports. Swatting is considered a serious criminal offense due to its potential to cause harm, endanger lives, and disrupt public safety.

- **Sycophants**: are individuals who excessively flatter and praise creators in order to gain personal benefits or favor. They wholeheartedly agree with and support the creator without questioning or offering any form of criticism, sometimes to the point of being insincere. The term is often used negatively to describe someone who lacks integrity and is willing to compromise their own principles in order to curry favor with the creators. Haters may employ this term to describe legitimately loyal fans of channels or individuals they dislike, insinuating that these fans blindly follow and praise someone seen as a public enemy, often without substantiating evidence.
- **Target (victim)**: person or group that is the subject of cyber-hatred.
- **Threats**: statements intended to cause fear, harm, or intimidation to the victim.
- **TOS**: refers to "Terms of Service" is a set of rules and guidelines that govern the use of a service, website, or application. They are typically created by the service provider to outline the user's responsibilities and obligations.
- **Tragedy pimps**: used for many years, particularly on social media platforms, to refer to individuals or organizations that take advantage of tragedy or suffering for their own personal gain or agenda. Often observed in the context of media coverage of tragic

events like natural disasters, terrorist attacks, or homicide. Instead of genuinely supporting the victims, their primary motive is to seek profit or other benefit from the situation.

- **Trolling**: deliberately posting rude, inflammatory, offensive, or disruptive messages online to provoke an emotional reaction from others. This is in line with "trolling armies" (cyber-mob, cyber-army) when groups of people do this to quickly magnify the damage.
- **Two-factor authentication (2FA)**: a security feature that requires users to provide two forms of identification to access their accounts, such as a password and a code sent to their phone or email.
- **Upstander**: a person who intervenes or speaks out against cyberbullying and other online attacks. They report abusive behavior, support the victim, and even share or create content as a way to spread public awareness.
- **Victim-blaming**: blaming the victim or survivor of harmful or traumatic events for what happened to them, instead of blaming the perpetrator.
- **Virtual private network (VPN)**: a pathway that encrypts internet traffic and provides online privacy and security by masking the user's IP address and location. Great for protecting you, but cyberbullies hide and evade consequences using this too.
- **Web filter**: software that blocks or restricts access to certain websites or content, often used by schools or workplaces to protect users.
- **XML (Extensible Markup Language)**: programming language used to store and transmit data.
- **Zero tolerance**: a policy that does not tolerate any form of cyberbullying, cyberhate, or online harassment, and takes immediate action to address any incidents that occur.

It's understandable that if you don't have a strong understanding of technology, some of these terms may seem confusing. While the list provided in the book covers everything needed for its purpose, it's worth noting that new words are consistently being created as the online landscape changes.

If you desire more clarification on any specific term, conducting an online search can be helpful. However, it's important to keep in mind that there may be some overlap among terms, which can further add to the confusion.

Art by Mozelle Martin
(www.VisualDiversity.art)

Thoughts & Insights:

Preface

In our interconnected world, cyber-hatred presents a menacing threat, lurking in the shadows, ready to launch venomous attacks on unsuspecting targets. This book seeks to illuminate the hidden corners of the internet, unraveling the intricate web of cyber-hatred that ensnares professional adults. By understanding the psychological complexities of cyber-haters, we can more effectively combat this destructive phenomenon (Goleman, 1995).

The Self-Esteem Movement Did Not Help:

The self-esteem movement, initially aimed at fostering confidence, has unintentionally fostered an environment of insecurity and vulnerability. Knowing this, perhaps it can urge readers to reassess the consequences of this movement since excessive emphasis on high self-esteem can result in a sense of entitlement, narcissism, and an inability to cope with criticism or failure (Jones, 2022).

Distinguishing Self-Esteem and Narcissism:

It is crucial to distinguish between genuine self-esteem, which emerges from authentic accomplishments, embracing personal values, and demonstrating empathy towards others, and narcissism, which originates from fear, self-centeredness, and a longing for superiority (Clarkson, 2021).

Parenting Practices for True Self-Esteem:

In Dr. Robert Firestone's book, *"The Self Under Siege,"* his insight underscores the significance of parents fostering the development of an authentic sense of self in their children. It provides guidance on adopting a balanced parenting approach that encompasses love, warmth, affection, attunement to a child's needs, and appropriate guidance, direction, and discipline.

While the primary focus of *this* book is on *adult* victims of cyber-hatred, it recognizes that the psychological and behavioral characteristics of adult cyber-haters often trace back to their childhood. This realization should then prompt independent researchers to explore the link between childhood experiences and the formation of cyber-hatred (Lee et al., 2020).

Independent Research & Critical Thinking:

In today's digital era, independent research and critical thinking skills are crucial for navigating both the virtual and physical realms. It is especially important to teach our youth the significance of these skills and provide them with valuable resources, links to research studies, references, and local examples to enhance their abilities in this area.

The Dark Triad, Tetrad, and Cyber-Hatred:

Extensive research has uncovered a substantial correlation between specific personality traits, commonly referred to as the dark triad or tetrad traits (D-traits), and the prevalence of cyber-hatred. This book delves into the psychological factors contributing to cyber-hatred, shedding light on the possible motivations and behaviors of individuals engaged in these detrimental activities (McCullough et al, 2003).

Research Findings:

This book also presents multiple studies that establish correlations between dark traits and concerning patterns of social media usage. It also investigates how aspects of narcissism and gender differences influence the choice of related social media platforms and behavior.

Prevalence of Cyber-Hatred:

According to www.Security.org, cyber-hatred is distributed across various social media platforms as follows: 79% on YouTube, 69% on Snapchat, 64% on TikTok, 49% on Facebook, and 41% on Twitter. These statistics underscore the widespread presence of cyber-hatred and serve as a stark reminder of its pervasive nature (O'Driscoll, 2023).

The Reality of Negative Feedback:

In the digital world we live in today, aspiring content creators must be prepared for the possibility of encountering negative feedback. This book provides valuable insights into the significant impact that negative comments can have on an individual's mental and physical well-being. It particularly focuses on offering guidance to sensitive individuals, urging them to carefully consider the decision of engaging with public platforms such as YouTube, which can expose them to elevated levels of cyber-hatred (Owaida, 2020). *We will delve deeper into this topic later in the book.*

Understanding Platform Guidelines:

This book emphasizes the crucial significance of adhering to community guidelines on all online platforms, even in cases where it may appear that the platform does not prioritize enforcement. It delves into the various forms of behavior that violate these guidelines, including harassment and bullying, and the potential consequences. Additionally, it offers valuable advice to content creators on how to avoid participating in toxic conduct.

Navigating the Digital Landscape:

This book provides readers with valuable guidance and resources, enhancing their comprehension of cyber-hatred and its consequences, particularly within professional adult contexts. It emphasizes the importance of exercising caution when interacting with individuals on social media platforms, especially those who claim expertise or exert influence. The book underscores the significance of conducting thorough research and adopting a skeptical mindset when confronted with unrealistic promises or claims.

Real-Life Experiences and Case Studies:

The book features brief case studies that highlight the real-life experiences of adult victims of cyber-hatred. These narratives aim to increase awareness about the widespread occurrence and detrimental effects of cyber-hatred. They also serve as proof that nobody is immune.

Research, Analysis, and Empowerment:

In addition to providing research findings, this book offers readers a comprehensive understanding of cyber-hatred and its extensive impact. Although addressing cyber-hatred comprehensively presents challenges, fostering empathy, encouraging dialogue, and promoting digital citizenship are crucial in creating a safer and more inclusive online environment for everyone (Patchin, 2020).

With these objectives in mind, this book serves as a foundation for understanding, combating, and navigating the shadows of cyber-hatred. Let us embark on this journey together.

"Oh, look who it is! It's our esteemed guest - the monster extraordinaire - firmly planted upon his computer throne. As the true hero of the internet, those eye bags are testaments to the countless hours he has devoted to spreading joy and enlightenment across the world. His uncanny prowess as a creep with a keyboard is nothing short of inspirational, defying all boundaries. Let us unite with unwavering admiration to pay homage to his unparalleled expertise in tormenting strangers online. Bravo!"

#MonsterMash   #SocialMediaMonsters
#CreepsWithKeyboards   #TrollGoals
#MonsterExtraordinaire   #InternetLegend

(sarcasm fully intended)

Thoughts & Insights:

My Cyber-Hatred Story

Instead of a conventional introduction, I will share my personal story in this section. This book is a direct outcome of my own experience, and it is vital to grasp the motivations behind its creation and its global significance. This will allow you to develop a deeper understanding of the content that follows.

If you are unfamiliar with me, allow me to summarize. I have amassed more than 35 years of experience as an international handwriting expert and forensic mental health professional primarily within correctional facilities. During my 14 years of college, I obtained multiple degrees in Criminology and Forensic Psychology. Additionally, I acquired a Certification in Crime Scene Investigation and completed a Ph.D. in Applied Ethics.

In my professional journey, I have established close collaborations with investigative agencies worldwide. This includes serving as an expert witness in questioned document cases. Additionally, I have offered handwriting analysis services and conducted training sessions to assess and identify personality traits for a wide range of clients. These clients encompass private individuals, Fortune 500 corporations, mental health professionals, educators, law enforcement agencies, and human resource departments for companies of various sizes.

As a conscientious YouTube creator, I have observed and personally encountered the detrimental effects of cyber-hatred. That's why it is important to clarify certain aspects of my YouTube channel before we proceed.

First, my channel is *not* categorized as a "true crime" and *never* has been. Furthermore, as I will soon reveal, my channel does *not* generate substantial income. Ultimately, the primary objective of my channel is to *entertain* viewers by providing insights into human behavior through the analysis of handwriting – what I call "deciphering the personality behind the pen."

Furthermore, throughout my short tenure as a creator, I have consistently emphasized to my subscribers the importance of conducting independent research. I always encourage them not to blindly accept information from just any ol' source, but to verify or experience it firsthand.

In our fast-paced society, where instant gratification is expected, many people have developed a habit of relying solely on their preferred creators without independently verifying the information they see or hear.

I hold the belief that creators bear an ethical responsibility to provide accurate information within their expertise and abilities. However, it is crucial to acknowledge that viewers hold the ultimate responsibility for employing critical thinking when consuming content. It is up to the viewers to actively conduct independent research, and evaluate information from various sources to ensure a well-informed understanding. By taking on this role, viewers can navigate the digital landscape more effectively to form independent conclusions.

I also firmly believe that creators should refrain from engaging in unethical behaviors such as instigating or inciting group mobbing, making false accusations, launching personal attacks, engaging in professional defamation, or spreading disinformation and misinformation. These activities are not only deeply unethical but can also have legal implications. Unfortunately, not all content creators uphold ethical standards, and some even participate in illegal activities.

Moreover, some creators unjustly project their own dissatisfaction with life onto unsuspecting individuals.

When creators engage in behaviors associated with cyber-hatred, such as cyberbullying, shunning, shaming, and other tactics explored in this book, they not only harm their own reputation but also contribute to the toxic online environment that pervades our society. By participating in such behaviors or similar ones, they perpetuate a harmful online culture that negatively impacts individuals and communities.

If you are familiar with me, you probably already know that I strongly believe platforms should bear the responsibility of maintaining a professional environment, rather than relying on private individuals to enforce the rules. This belief stems from the observation that many individuals lack integrity and often act impulsively, driven by their emotions. That's why platforms should take proactive measures to address and prevent misconduct, rather than turning a blind eye to such incidents.

By rightfully taking on this responsibility, platforms can contribute to the creation of a safer and more responsible online space for all users. This entails implementing measures to identify and address instances of misconduct, establishing transparent guidelines and policies for user behavior, and employing effective moderation and enforcement mechanisms. Through these actions, platforms play a vital role in promoting a professional and respectful online environment.

Now, I would like to share my personal experience...

I started my Vimeo channel in 2006 but eventually switched to YouTube due to changes on the platform that didn't align with my preferences. Initially, my main purpose for using these platforms was to securely store files for my children and grandchildren, ensuring their preservation long after I passed away. This was before I was familiar with the concept of "cloud" storage, so it was crucial for me to keep my content safe, especially after experiencing multiple computer crashes that resulted in the unfortunate loss of important files. During that time, I had no intention or desire to actively participate as a "creator" on either Vimeo or YouTube, and my personal engagement with content on both platforms was extremely minimal.

Everything changed in August 2022.

While on a business trip, I had a intriguing encounter with a retired detective who happened to host a true crime channel on YouTube. During a group lunch, he showed me an unknown handwriting sample on his phone, which caught my attention. I offered a spontaneous analysis, leading to a lively discussion. Interested in my insights, the detective proposed featuring the analysis in a video for his show, and I enthusiastically agreed.

The detective cautioned me about the possibility of facing harassment from other creators within the true crime community if I were to appear on his show, describing it as a "blood sport." While I acknowledged his warning, I didn't dwell on it extensively since my own channel had a different purpose, goal, and overall genre, which made it distinct from the true crime niche. In fact, as I explained to my husband, *"There are nearly 8 billion people in the world and over 50 million YouTube channels, so there should be plenty of space for everyone."*

However, being someone with autism, I found it challenging to comprehend the dynamics behind the existence of drama, hatred, and toxicity among YouTube channels or content creators in the first place. The concept of engaging in such negative behaviors seemed puzzling, unprofessional, and completely illogical to me.

After my appearance on the detective's show, I started receiving messages from anonymous YouTube creators who purported to warn me about said detective. However, these individuals did not disclose their real names, and I had no information about their credibility. They emailed me links to videos discussing specific names and cases related to true crime, including a few that mentioned the detective. It was all perplexing for me since I was unfamiliar with the other individuals in the videos and had never followed true crime content before.

In an attempt to gain clarity, I briefly watched the videos. Unfortunately, they only deepened my confusion and overwhelmed me, exacerbating my autism symptoms. Realizing the importance of prioritizing my well-being, I engaged in immediate self-care and completely gave up on trying to comprehend the situation.

Reluctant to admit my lack of understanding and overwhelm to strangers, I responded respectfully stating that I appreciated the heads up but that I form my own opinions based on personal interactions, not on someone else's perception. I made it clear that I am only responsible for my own actions and that any bias against the detective was of no relevance to me. Additionally, I mentioned that I would proceed cautiously due to my involvement with other experts within the same agency, acknowledging the importance of maintaining professional relationships.

Of course, as expected, these unknown individuals claimed my verbiage was because I sided *with* them. In reality, I was treading carefully *because* of them. I mean, if they are sending this type of hate-filled content *to* me (someone they don't know at all), just imagine what they could send to others *about* me.

Nothing more was said until...

Approximately a month later, the same detective sent me another handwriting sample from an unknown person. Despite my lack of knowledge or interest in the case or the individual who wrote the sample, I agreed to make another appearance on his YouTube show, just like I had done previously.

As a side note, I want to emphasize that throughout my extensive 35-year career working with international investigative agencies, I have never felt the need to request case details or information about the writer of a document. Such information has always been irrelevant to me since the handwriting itself provides all the necessary information I need to know.

The official beginning of my story unfolded when two significant events occurred: (1) I made the decision to finally start a YouTube show for my adult son, who had gently urged me to do so for many years, and (2) I extended a professional courtesy by inviting the detective to appear on my show. This invitation was in recognition of the fact that he had featured me on his show and had played a significant role in jumpstarting the majority of subscribers on my channel. However, shortly after conducting the interview with the detective on my show, I found myself becoming the target of cyber-hatred, experiencing deliberate and focused online attacks.

Initially, my haters criticized me for not vetting the detective before he appeared on my show. I firmly believed that it wasn't my responsibility to conduct a thorough background check on him, just as it isn't my duty to vet my own medical doctor. I assumed that law enforcement agencies had already performed their due diligence in working with him, just as a hospital would do before hiring my doctor.

Despite the cyber-hatred directed at me, I chose to disregard it. However, the situation escalated when the same strangers who initially reached out to me said, *"We tried to warn you when we sent you the videos, but you didn't listen. Now you'll have to pay the social consequences."*

Almost immediately, their warning seemed to fuel even more frequent and vicious attacks from other cyber-haters (their sycophants). In other words, these haters, monsters, and creeps targeted me because I didn't align myself with their perspective. By refusing to take their side, I became a prime target for their relentless and ongoing attacks.

If you are familiar with the true crime community on YouTube, this might not come as a surprise, but I was shocked.

When their initial approach did not yield the desired outcome, it appeared that the cyber-haters shifted their focus to attacking me based on allegations that my content lacked a disclaimer. However, their accusations were baseless, as I had consistently included an *"entertainment disclaimer"* beneath every video for over 10 years. Additionally, I had prominent disclaimers on my channel's 'About' page and video trailer. Despite my efforts to provide clarity and transparency, these attackers disregarded the evidence and instead chose to jump on the bandwagon without verifying the facts firsthand.

If these individuals had employed critical thinking and conducted basic independent research, they would have seen or heard the explicit statements in my videos emphasizing that *"nothing should be taken as 100% fact."* This statement clearly indicated that my content was not intended to present absolute truths. Unfortunately, their lack of diligence and their willingness to jump to conclusions led them to overlook these crucial disclaimers.

In summary, instead of acknowledging their lack of diligence, these individuals launched unwarranted attacks against me. They refused to take responsibility for their inactions, errors in judgment, and lack of independent thinking skills, instead directing their anger towards me.

NOBODY DESERVES TO BE VICTIMIZED...

Throughout the 10 years with my Vimeo and YouTube channels, these monsters and creeps were nowhere to be found. It was only after appearing on the detective's show that they appeared in my life, just as he had warned me.

I want to make it clear that I am not assigning any blame to the detective for the attacks I endured. It seems that the individuals who targeted me utilized a "guilt by association" tactic, directing their attacks towards various experts who were associated with the detective. The statement I mentioned earlier, where they warned me about *"paying the social consequences,"* further supports this observation. It is important to understand that although the detective and I are not close friends, he has consistently treated me with respect, and I have no concerns about our professional relationship.

After their initial attempts failed, my attackers sought another avenue to target me. It seems that they had a strong dislike for my chosen career field. However, I want to emphasize that their opinion of graphology or handwriting analysis holds no significance to me. I am confident in my chosen profession and will not allow their criticisms to undermine my passion and dedication.

It is important to address the fact that their repeated assertions of these attacks being mere "academic disagreements" do not excuse or justify the personal assaults they launched against me. Their unfounded labeling of me as a *liar, fraud, charlatan, grifter, tragedy pimp,* and others goes beyond the boundaries of legitimate criticism. It violates the principles of truth, reason, fairness, and ethics.

If, by any chance, my haters come across this book, I would like to clarify the distinctions between a genuine academic disagreement and a personal attack, as it seems they are confused about the two.

- **Academic disagreements** act as the lifeblood for fueling the exploration of diverse perspectives. By expressing differing opinions, presenting well-constructed counter-arguments, and engaging in *respectful* debates, we create an environment that *nurtures* collaboration. The convergence of diverse viewpoints helps us delve deeper into complex issues and *expands* our boundaries of knowledge thereby *encouraging* intellectual growth and *inspiring* creativity. This type of 'disagreement' is about a *topic*, not a human being.
- **Personal attacks** are like a *destructive* wildfire within discussions. Rather than addressing the substance of an argument, their personal attacks target a *human being* thereby attempting to undermine their victim's credibility and *devalue* the contribution of their victims. These attacks are marked by *derogatory* remarks, *insults*, and an *absence* of thoughtful engagement. Not only do personal attacks *impede* prolific conversations,

but they also *create hostility, erode* trust, and *hinder* the exploration of diverse viewpoints.

As you delve deeper into this book, you will likely arrive at the same conclusion as I have: the individuals I identify as the *Social Media Monsters* and *Creeps with Keyboards* have blatantly disregarded the ethical principles of "academic disagreements." Instead, they have chosen to engage in personal attacks against me and their other victims. I have full confidence that as you continue reading, you will notice their patterns and motives becoming increasingly evident.

It is truly puzzling that these individuals, often hiding behind usernames and profile avatars (cartoons), believe they are entitled to an explanation for my chosen career path. However, just as I didn't feel the need to explain my career choice to my parents, children, or spouse, I certainly don't owe complete strangers an explanation for my actions.

And neither do you.

My career path is a personal decision that I have made based on my interests, skills, and passion, and I stand by that choice without the need for external validation or approval, especially from hateful and anonymous people.

Following the advice of my legal team, I chose to ignore all haters, monsters, and creeps starting in mid-November 2022, just three days after the cyber-attacks began. For ten months prior to my experience, I had been transferring my Vimeo content to YouTube and had scheduled content to be randomly auto-published over the next two years.

Despite my efforts to disengage from these malicious monsters, they persisted in their hateful behavior. They responded with more vicious content in various forms, including videos, audio recordings, and written material, whenever one of my pre-scheduled videos was released. This ongoing harassment served as a constant reminder of their relentless determination to attack and undermine me, even though I had chosen not to engage with them.

These retaliations included unfounded and childish claims that the specific pre-scheduled video was intentionally directed at them. However, these accusations hold no validity because, had they taken the time to read the video description or listen to the content, they would have realized that the videos originated as far back as 2007. Let me provide two examples to illustrate this point:

Handwriting Analysis: Analyzing 13 Famous People Mozelle Martin analyzes the handwriting of stars such as Sylvia Browne, Lindsay Lohan, Britney Spears, Paula Abdul, Michael...	© Public	Apr 2, 2007 Published
Handwriting Analysis: My Most Memorable Cases What were Mozelle Martin's most memorable cases? Find out this and more on this segment. This is from 2010. ►►To help you	© Public	Apr 2, 2007 Published

Starting in 2015, I have made it a habit to disconnect from the internet during the entire month of December. This intentional break enables me to focus on important tasks such as updating my website and biography, fulfilling holiday orders, and wrapping up ongoing projects like books or commissioned artwork. Moreover, it serves as a self-care practice that helps me navigate the symptoms associated with my autism and multiple sclerosis. By taking this time off, I am able to prioritize my overall well-being and effectively manage the challenges that arise from these conditions, as well as the sensory overload commonly experienced during the holiday season.

Unfortunately, the monsters and creeps falsely claimed that my decision to go offline and make changes to my website and biography was influenced by *their* hateful and vicious attacks, suggesting that I had something to hide.

To refute these baseless claims once again, I created a video presenting screenshots from each year since 2015. These screenshots provide visual proof that I indeed disconnected from the internet during that specific timeframe, thereby debunking any baseless assumptions made against me.

Here is an example of one of the screenshots...

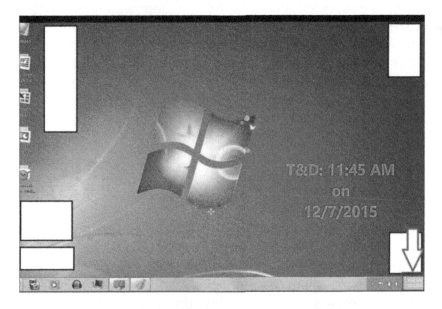

Ironically, everything they accused me of doing to them was actually what they were doing to me.

In essence, the accusations made *against* me by these individuals were a reflection of their own actions *toward* me. The crucial distinction lies in *their* misguided belief that they could provide evidence to contradict me, whereas the truth was that *I* had already repeatedly disproven their claims.

These individuals purposefully spread false information and deceived their followers, perpetuating an ongoing cycle of negativity and hostility. It is important to note that my haters openly admitted their intentions, stating, *"When I encourage them to take action, my subscribers grasp my message. I don't need to provide explicit instructions because they already know what needs to be done."*

As a result of this message, a considerable number of their followers promptly began harassing me, with several resorting to extreme measures. Furthermore, some of their associates went to the extent of creating videos and short clips that specifically targeted me, rather than just asking me about my career.

In my view, their attacks were clearly aimed at undermining both my personal character and professional reputation, indicating that it was a personal grudge rather than a legitimate academic disagreement. It is possible that the vendetta was primarily directed at the detective, and my experience was collateral damage. I have to ask your opinion... *are these monsters and creeps brave or stupid for targeting law enforcement officers?*

As a part of my research for this book, I took the initiative to establish private connections with certain individuals who were responsible for the harassment. In order to combat the hateful attacks directed towards me, I devised a strategy to *humanize* myself to those who were spreading the hate. Drawing upon my expertise in forensic psychology, I made a conscious decision to selectively disclose certain personal details that I had already made public through various mediums, including audio, video, and written content through the years.

These disclosures were carefully chosen and intended to serve as a catalyst to inspire the monsters and creeps to examine their own lives and behaviors even though I doubted it would work.

Given that these individuals had not bothered to watch my content since they missed my disclaimers, I was confident that they were oblivious to the fact that I had already made these personal details publicly available. Keeping in mind what I believe to be their narcissistic tendencies, I anticipated that they would interpret my disclosures as a sign of personal trust and a desire to establish a friendship with them. I knew that in doing so, it would feed their ego and satisfy their need for validation and importance.

One of the things I disclosed was that *I made mistakes, such as becoming a mother at a young age (21) and potentially not giving my children the attention that they needed due to the hyper-focus on my career.*

I also disclosed that *I have never intentionally harmed anyone. On the contrary, I have always gone above and beyond to help others, even though it hasn't always worked out as intended.*

I explained that, *throughout my 25-year career in mental health, I served as a trauma therapist and that early in my career, I learned a crucial lesson about the importance of teaching, encouraging, and inspiring individuals to help themselves. Some people tend to thrive in misery and drama, preferring to complain. Despite their words, deep down, they either lack a genuine desire for change or deliberately refuse to put in the necessary effort.*

Next, I shared that *the fundamental issue is that if these individuals truly created a fulfilling life for themselves, what would they have to complain about? This resistance also becomes an obstacle for anyone trying to assist them, as it can lead to codependency and emotional exhaustion.*

I was also thinking that if my haters had a life they enjoyed, they wouldn't feel the need to create hate.

I then explained that, *when someone's expectations don't align with reality, disappointment arises. I had to learn that if people are not willing to help themselves, the best course of action for me is to step back and do nothing. This often meant walking away, hoping that they will find their own path and discover fulfillment.*

I told them that, *although it can be difficult not to feel guilty for letting go, as long as I know I have done my best, it becomes easier. However, if I don't detach myself soon enough, it can prolong their misery and negatively affect my own well-being.*

By sharing personal stories like these to earn their trust and stroke their egos, it seemed to have worked. Shortly afterward, I received private messages stating, *"We will stop talking about you, and once we announce this to our viewers, no more action will be taken against you. We actually think you are a nice person and would be more likely to defend you now."*

Humanizing myself yielded the desired outcome and provided written proof. However, I strongly advise against attempting this unless you have the necessary education, training, and skills to support you. Now that I have documented it, if they decide to resume their hateful tactics toward me, it will only further damage *their* public image and *their* reputation, which narcissists despise and try to avoid at all costs.

Although the attacks against me have ceased, it is important to note that the hateful content still remains public as I write this. While I consider myself fortunate that my experience was relatively short-lived, it deeply troubles me to witness others enduring much longer campaigns, sometimes lasting years.

The lack of public awareness and support for adult professionals facing cyber-hatred is also deeply concerning. The insufficient resources available to professionals in similar situations is disheartening.

From my perspective, there is an immediate and pressing need to establish support systems that specifically cater to the distinctive challenges faced by adult victims of cyber-hatred. Additionally, many older adults lack the essential technical skills and guidance to navigate through these distressing experiences, highlighting the importance of having advocates who can support and assist them during such times.

I am also concerned about the apparent inaction from social media platforms, including YouTube. When offensive content is reported, it often doesn't receive a satisfactory response. It seems that YouTube prioritizes sensational content to boost their viewership and profits, disregarding their own terms of service and anti-harassment policies. This further victimizes individuals who are already being targeted by other creators and viewers.

While I use YouTube as a primary example, I believe that no platform is immune to ignoring reports and online attacks. As you will discover, most, if not all, platforms have their own issues.

Meanwhile, research has shown that individuals who engage in hateful behavior often exhibit high levels of psychopathology and sadism. I will explore this topic further in detail later on. It is crucial to acknowledge that these individuals participate in disrespectful conversations, manipulate words, and incite hatred for their personal gain.

As an example, one of my haters went to great lengths to damage my reputation by using deceptive tactics. This person took my YouTube logo and created a fake account to leave comments on another hater's channel, making it seem like I was actively participating in a "live" event, attempting to defend myself. It's important to emphasize that during this incident, I was with federal agents and police officers of which at least two individuals sitting right next to me during dinner witnessed the comments being made in the chatroom. These individuals can testify that I had no involvement in those comments.

This experience emphasizes the importance of providing support to victims and holding platforms like YouTube, Vimeo, Facebook, Twitter, TikTok, WhatsApp, and others accountable for their actions.

Years ago, I proposed to YouTube the implementation of a vetting policy similar to Twitter's blue checkmark system. Such a policy could instill trust and confidence among creators and their viewers, particularly in the true crime genre, where lives can be impacted and cases can be compromised. Unsolved crimes, disinformation, and misinformation have the potential to create more victims, tarnish the reputations of innocent individuals, and jeopardize public safety.

As I contemplate my motivations for writing this book, I acknowledge that they stem from a combination of personal and professional factors. Even without personal experience in cyberhatred, I believe that increasing public awareness in a society plagued by hatred and division is crucial.

With that in mind, this book serves as a platform for launching a supportive public awareness campaign, aiming to achieve the following goals:

• **Creating a culture of respect**: is important to educate individuals about the impact of their online actions, promote diverse perspectives, and encourage harmonious interactions.

• **Cybersecurity**: to educate individuals about the risks associated with cyberbullying and promote safe online behaviors by raising awareness.

• **Economic costs**: to showcase the significant economic implications, including emotional distress, decreased productivity, and long-term consequences for victims.

• **Education**: to discourage harmful behavior, promote reporting and support-seeking, and cultivate a culture of empathy.

• **Encouraging responsible technology use**: to promote responsible usage, critical thinking, and online ethics.

• **Global impact**: to bring together individuals, organizations, and government agencies to counteract cyberbullying on a global scale.

• **Increased empathy**: to encourage respectful behavior. By helping individuals understand the emotional impact of cyberbullying, these campaigns can shape future social norms and contribute to a more compassionate society.

• **Intervention**: to empower victims to seek help and bystanders to intervene, thereby fostering a supportive environment that discourages harmful behavior and leads to prevention.

• **Legal action**: to influence laws and policies by raising awareness of cyberbullying's severity and consequences.

• **Mental health**: to highlight the impact of cyberbullying, promote support-seeking, and combat the stigma.

• **Protection of vulnerable groups**: for marginalized individuals by educating the public about cyberbullying that specifically targets these groups. This will then promote inclusivity and acceptance.

• **Reputation management**: to equip individuals with strategies to protect their reputation from cyber-haters.

• **Support**: for victims by creating a sense of community, sharing stories of resilience, and offering resources.

By sharing information about the experiences of targeted adult professionals, we can highlight the severity of these incidents and avoid perpetuating the problem through ignorance (Twenge, 2014). Engaging in open discussions helps the public understand the unique challenges faced by these individuals online, fostering empathy and compassion. Increased awareness also enables the development of preventive measures and support systems.

With awareness comes action. When individuals are aware of the harm caused by cyberbullying and targeted attacks, they are more likely to take action and become advocates for change (Twenge, 2014). They can push for policies that protect victims and hold perpetrators accountable. Through collective efforts, we can create a virtual society where such incidents occur less frequently, and individuals feel safe, respected, and valued.

Art by Mozelle Martin
(www.VisualDiversity.art)

Defining Cyber-Hatred

To align with the overall theme of this book, it is crucial to define the primary subject of focus, which is cyber-hatred.

Cyber-hatred refers to the expression of intense animosity, hostility, or prejudice through online platforms like social media, forums, or messaging apps (Smith et al., 2018). It involves using digital communication tools to spread hateful messages, engage in harassment, and target individuals or groups based on their race, religion, gender, sexual orientation, nationality, or other distinguishing characteristics (Johnson, 2020).

Cyber-hatred often manifests as cyberbullying, where individuals exploit the anonymity and distance afforded by the internet to intentionally harm, intimidate, or demean others (Brown et al., 2019). This harmful behavior can take various forms, including spreading hateful comments, making threats, sharing false information, creating fake profiles, hacking, doxing, and organizing online campaigns to promote their hateful agenda (Clarkson, 2021).

The motivations behind cyber-hatred are diverse and can stem from personal biases, ignorance, political or ideological extremism, seeking attention or amusement, or simply the desire to cause harm and distress (Smith et al., 2018). Surprisingly, research suggests that 45% of individuals engaging in hateful trolling do so solely for entertainment purposes (Johnson, 2020).

However, cyber-hatred has significant consequences. It leads to psychological distress, reputational harm, loss of privacy, financial insecurity, and, in extreme cases, physical or self-inflicted harm (Brown et al., 2019; Clarkson, 2021). Therefore, the primary objective of this book is to address the issue of cyber-hatred in a distinct manner compared to existing publications.

Effectively navigating the realm of social media, which is inhabited by malevolent individuals and keyboard creeps, necessitates a comprehensive approach involving education, awareness, policy implementation, and the use of technological tools (Smith et al., 2018). By adopting this multifaceted approach, we can strive to combat cyber-hatred and create a safer online environment.

"Who needs social skills when you can so easily terrorize others within the digital realm?"

#MonsterTechMaster   (sarcasm fully intended)

Thoughts & Insights:

Thoughts & Insights:

Types of Cyber-Haters

In the era of widespread communication, it is clear that both positive and negative aspects thrive. To provide insight into the prevalent online negativity, let me introduce you to some common types of online haters. It is important to note that this list is not exhaustive as new tactics constantly emerge in response to the ever-evolving online landscape (Davis et al., 2016).

1. **Ableist**: targets individuals with disabilities through derogatory or discriminatory comments or behaviors.
2. **Ageist**: directs derogatory or discriminatory comments or behaviors toward individuals of different age groups.
3. **Anonymous attacker**: conceals his identity behind anonymous or fake profiles to engage in negative behavior without facing consequences.
4. **Attention seeker**: craves validation and attention from others and resorts to negative behavior like posting inflammatory comments or starting arguments to elicit emotional responses.
5. **Body shamer**: engages in negative behavior aimed at someone's physical appearance to make victims feel ashamed or inferior.
6. **Bored provocateur**: instigates trouble or seeks reactions from others by engaging in negative behavior solely for the sake of causing disruption.
7. **Catfisher**: creates fake profiles and assumes false identities to deceive or manipulate others.
8. **Conspiracy theorist**: motivated by a belief in conspiracy theories, he engages in negative behavior to defend or promote his views.
9. **Copycat**: emulates negative behaviors of others without fully considering the impact of his actions; often influenced by the creators he follows and supports.
10. **Cyberbully**: deliberately targets and harasses specific individuals, engaging in actions such as spreading

rumors, making threats or derogatory comments, intimidation, and sharing of personal information.

11. **Disinformation spreader**: intentionally spreads false or misleading information, such as rumors, collusions, or fake news to manipulate others.

12. **Do-gooder-gone-bad**: initially driven by good intentions or a desire to promote a cause, he eventually exhibits toxic or abusive behaviors. This pattern is often observed among those labeled as "bible thumpers" or "zealots", "conspiracy theorists", and "political sensationalists."

13. **Doomsayer**: spreads fear, uncertainty, or doubt by engaging in negative behavior driven by a sense of impending doom.

14. **Doxxer**: publicly shares an individual's personal information without their consent, including their full name, address, phone number, and other sensitive details.

15. **Elitist**: motivated by a sense of superiority or exclusivity, he engages in negative behavior to demean or belittle those he considers inferior.

16. **Enabler**: encourages or enables negative behavior in others by liking, commenting, or sharing negative content.

17. **Fan person**: exhibits negative behavior to defend his preferred "team" or attack competitors. He often does so as a fan of a particular celebrity, brand, or product.

18. **Gaslighter**: engages in behaviors intended to make the target doubt their own reality or perception of events.

19. **Gatekeeper**: motivated by a sense of authority or control, he engages in negative behavior to exclude or silence others who don't meet his standards.

20. **Grammar police**: obsessed with correcting others' grammar, spelling, or punctuation, he engages in negative behaviors to shame or belittle the perceived mistakes.

21. **Homophobe**: targets individuals who identify as LGBTQIA+ with derogatory or discriminatory comments.

22. **Ideological extremist**: motivated by deeply-held beliefs, he aggressively promotes his views or attacks

those who disagree with him through offensive or aggressive behavior.

23. **Impulsive hater**: engages in negative behaviors without considering the consequences. His actions are often driven by emotions rather than reason.

24. **Influencer hater**: motivated by jealousy or resentment towards social media influencers, celebrities, or public figures, he engages in negative behaviors to bring them down or tarnish their reputation.

25. **Jealous critic**: driven by envy, he engages in negative behavior to undermine or damage others' reputations.

26. **Keyboard warrior (creep)**: he is aggressive or confrontational in online interactions but does not exhibit the same behavior in face-to-face or IRL interactions.

27. **Know-it-all**: motivated by a sense of superiority or expertise, he engages in negative behaviors to belittle those he considers ignorant.

28. **Machiavellian**: uses online platforms to pursue various goals such as feeding his need for power, attention, or financial gain. He employs deceptive tactics like creating fake profiles or using pseudonyms to manipulate others while projecting a false image.

29. **Misogynist**: targets women with misogynistic comments or behaviors to intimidate or silence them.

30. **Passive hater**: does not actively engage in negative behavior but his lack of support for victims can be hurtful.

31. **Passive-aggressive hater**: exhibits negative behavior in subtle or indirect ways, such as through sarcasm or passive-aggressive comments.

32. **Plagiarist**: copies or steals content from others without proper attribution, often for self-promotion or personal agenda.

33. **Political extremist**: driven by strong political views, he engages in negative behaviors to promote his ideologies or attack those with differing opinions.

34. **Racial or cultural bigot**: motivated by prejudice or discrimination based on race, ethnicity, or cultural background, he employs derogatory comments, slurs, offensive language, and behaviors.

35. **Revenge seeker**: motivated by a desire for revenge, he engages in negative behaviors to retaliate against those he perceives as having wronged him.

36. **Shock jock**: aims to shock or offend others by using negative behavior to gain attention or publicity (same as with cyber-drama).

37. **Troll**: purposefully posts provocative or offensive comments to elicit strong reactions from others.

38. **Troll farmer**: this is not an individual, but rather, an organized group using social media and other online platforms to spread misinformation or propaganda to influence public opinion or disrupt social discourse.

39. **Victim blamer**: targets those who have experienced trauma, such as sexual assault or harassment, with victim-blaming comments.

40. **Zealot**: driven by extreme or fanatical commitments to particular ideologies, religions, or belief systems, he engages in negative behaviors to defend or promote his views.

Art by Mozelle Martin
(www.VisualDiversity.art)

Thoughts & Insights:

Cyber-Hater Tactics

Cyberhatred encompasses a wide range of tactics and strategies used by individuals to harass, intimidate, or harm others in online environments (Hall, 2022). These tactics exploit different digital platforms and communication tools, specifically targeting victims and causing them considerable losses and / or psychological distress (Hussain et al, 2020).

Outlined below are the six most prevalent tactics employed by individuals of malicious intent (Brown et al., 2019; Johnson, 2020):

1. Harassment and Threats:

- Sending repeated offensive or threatening messages, emails, or comments.
- Directly targeting individuals with harmful, demeaning, or derogatory language.
- Posting or sharing explicit or humiliating content about the victim.

2. Social Exclusion and Rumor Spreading:

- Excluding the victim from online groups, chats, or social circles.
- Spreading false rumors, gossip, or misinformation about the victim.
- Manipulating others to ostracize or isolate the victim online.

3. Impersonation and Identity Theft:

- Creating fake profiles or accounts to impersonate the victim.
- Stealing personal information and using it to harass or defame the victim.

- Utilizing hacked accounts to spread malicious content in the victim's name.

4. Cyberstalking and Doxing:

- Persistent and intrusive monitoring of the victim's online activities.
- Collecting and sharing the victim's personal information without consent (doxing).
- Following, tracking, or digitally surveilling the victim's movements or interactions.

5. Online Shaming and Public Humiliation:

- Posting embarrassing photos, videos, or content about the victim.
- Encouraging others to ridicule or mock the victim publicly.
- Manipulating or distorting the victim's statements or actions to provoke shame.

6. Exclusionary and Hateful Communities:

- Involving the victim in hate groups or forums without their consent.
- Encouraging others to participate in hate speech or targeted harassment.
- Promoting discriminatory ideologies and fostering a toxic online environment.

It is essential to recognize that cyber-hatred tactics can overlap, combine, and adapt alongside advancements in technology and online platforms. Familiarity with these tactics is pivotal for identifying and addressing instances of cyber-hatred while providing support to victims and fostering a safer online environment (Martin et al, 2021).

"Move over, humans!
I'm the reigning champion of online creeping."

#MonsterTechAddict

(sarcasm fully intended)

While some of the other victims targeted by my haters chose to respond by calling them out on their channels and posts, I made a conscious decision not to engage in what I consider unethical or unprofessional behavior. From my perspective, the act of targeting and badmouthing others reveals more about the one doing the comments (aka "hating") than it does about the victim they are trying to target.

In my particular situation, it seemed that my haters were accustomed to the responses of other victims and assumed that I would react in the same manner. However, that did not happen. Furthermore, if I had responded in kind, it would have only generated more views, clicks, and financial gain for them. Therefore, I believe that in an attempt to deflect attention away from their own hateful behavior, the monsters and creeps resorted to falsely attributing negative actions to me, even though I did not engage in any such behavior.

Given my background and expertise in applied ethics, I believe it is important to acknowledge that individuals who possess both intelligence and malicious intentions often employ philosophical tactics to advance their agendas. With the assistance of Singer (2011), I will outline the most common philosophical accusations used.

- **A posteriori**: A proposition that is known to be true based on empirical evidence or experience. *"The sun rose this morning."* We can confidently say that occurred because we witnessed it directly or have proof that others also observed it. It relies on empirical evidence and is derived from sensory perception or data collected through experiments or observations.
- **A priori**: A proposition that is known to be true based on reason alone, independent of experience. *"All bachelors are unmarried."* This knowledge is

independent of experience or observation and is true based on logical reasoning alone.

- **Absolutism**: A moral or political theory that holds that certain principles or values are universally valid and applicable, regardless of cultural or historical context. A true philosophical absolutist might argue that moral principles such as *"killing innocent people is always wrong"* or *"truth is preferable to falsehood"* are universally true and valid in all circumstances, regardless of cultural or individual beliefs.
- **Absurdism**: A philosophy that emphasizes the meaningless and irrationality of human existence. For an example of this, read the essay "The Myth of Sisyphus" and the novel "The Stranger."
- **Ad Hominem (Abusive)**: This fallacy is a personal attack on the character or motives of a person making an argument, rather than addressing the argument itself. *"You're just a liar and a cheat, so your argument can't be trusted."*
- **Ad Hominem (Tu Quoque)**: This fallacy is an attempt to discredit an argument by accusing the person making the argument of hypocrisy or inconsistency. *"You can't say anything about honesty when you lied on your taxes last year."*
- **Ad Hominem**: Attacking the character or motive of an opponent, rather than addressing the substance of their argument. *"You can't trust my opponent because he's a known liar."* In other words, attacking the person making an argument, rather than addressing the argument itself. *"You can't trust him, he's a convicted criminal,"* or *"You can't trust John's argument about climate change, he's not even a scientist."*
- **Ad Populum**: Claiming that something is true simply because a large number of people believe it to be true. *"Everyone knows that you can't trust politicians."*
- **Aesthetics**: encompasses the study of beauty, taste, and the sensory and emotional experiences

associated with art, nature, and other objects of aesthetic appreciation. It examines how these experiences are created, perceived, and valued, and how they contribute to our understanding and enjoyment of the world around us.

- **Agnosticism**: A philosophical position that holds that the existence of God or other ultimate realities cannot be known or proven. *"I don't know if God or gods exist, and I don't believe it is possible to know for certain."*

- **Alienation**: A concept used in Marxist philosophy to describe the feeling of disconnection or estrangement that individuals experience in capitalist societies, whether from oneself, others, or society. This is often associated with modern industrial society.

- **Ambiguity**: Using unclear or vague language to make an argument. *"We need to reduce crime. Therefore, we need to take action."* Another example would be a sentence that can be interpreted in multiple ways due to its unclear or multiple meanings such as "I saw her duck." Was duck a verb or a bird?

- **Analytic philosophy**: A philosophical tradition that emphasizes the use of logical analysis and clarity of language in philosophical inquiry.

- **Anarchism**: A political philosophy that advocates for the elimination of all forms of government and the establishment of a society based on voluntary cooperation and mutual aid.

- **Anecdotal Fallacy**: Relying on personal anecdotes rather than data or evidence to support an argument. *"My grandfather smoked every day of his life and he lived to be 100, so smoking can't be that bad for you."*

- **Animal Ethics**: The branch of ethics that examines the moral and ethical implications of human interactions with non-human animals, and seeks to promote animal welfare and rights.

- **Appeal to Authority**: Arguing that something is true or acceptable because an authority figure says so, without providing sufficient evidence. *"The doctor said vaccines are safe, so they must be,"* or *"I believe in climate change because Al Gore said it's real,"* or *"I know the doctor said I need to lose weight, but my favorite celebrity says you should love yourself just the way you are,"* or, *"My doctor says that homeopathy works, so it must be true."*

- **Appeal to Antiquity**: The appeal to antiquity is a logical fallacy that relies on the age or acceptance of an idea to assume its truth or superiority. This fallacy overlooks evidence, logic, and progress in knowledge, and fails to provide a solid foundation for evaluating the validity of a claim. It is important to evaluate ideas based on their own merits, supported by reasoning and evidence. While historical context and traditions can offer insights, they should not be the sole basis for accepting or rejecting ideas. Critical thinking and open-mindedness are essential for advancing our understanding of the world beyond the age of an idea.

- **Appeal to Consequences**: Arguing that a claim must be true or false based on whether the consequences of accepting or rejecting it are desirable. *"If we stop using fossil fuels, it will destroy the economy, so we should keep using them."*

- **Appeal to Emotion**: Using emotions, rather than facts or evidence, to persuade or convince someone. *"You should support animal rights because think of all the poor, defenseless animals suffering,"* or *"If you care about the children, you'll support this legislation,"* or *"If we don't pass this bill, the world will end."*

- **Appeal to Ignorance**: Arguing that something is true simply because there is no evidence to prove it isn't. *"There's no evidence that aliens exist, so they must not be real,"* or *"No one has proven that Bigfoot doesn't exist, so it must be real."*

- **Appeal to Nature**: This fallacy is the argument that because something is natural, it must be good or right.

"Herbal remedies are better than pharmaceutical drugs because they are natural."

- **Appeal to Tradition**: Arguing that something is true or acceptable because it has been done a certain way for a long time. *"We have always celebrated Thanksgiving this way, so why change it?"*
- **Argument from Abduction**: The argument that the best explanation for a given phenomenon is the one that best accounts for the available evidence.
- **Argument from Analogy**: The argument that two things that are similar in some respects are likely to be similar in other respects, and that this similarity can be used to infer knowledge.
- **Argument from Animal Rights**: The argument that non-human animals have moral rights that should be recognized and respected by humans.
- **Argument from Authority**: Accepting something as true simply because an authority figure says it is true. *"The president said we need to invade that country, so it must be the right thing to do."*
- **Argument from Beauty**: The argument that the beauty and harmony of the natural world imply the existence of a creator.
- **Argument from Consciousness**: The argument that the existence of subjective experience and consciousness is evidence of a non-physical aspect of reality.
- **Argument from Consensus**: The argument that a knowledge claim is justified because it is widely accepted by a community of experts or scholars.
- **Argument from Contingency**: The argument that everything that exists is contingent, and that this implies the existence of a necessary being.
- **Argument from Cosmological Existence**: The argument that the existence of the universe requires an explanation or cause, which is God.

- **Argument from Deduction**: The argument that knowledge claims based on deductive reasoning (i.e., conclusions that follow logically from premises) are certain and infallible.
- **Argument from Deontology**: The argument that the morality of an action is determined by its conformity to moral rules or duties.
- **Argument from Design**: The argument that the complexity and order in the natural world imply the existence of an intelligent designer.
- **Argument from Desire**: The argument that our innate desire for happiness and fulfillment can only be satisfied by God.
- **Argument from Empiricism**: The argument that all knowledge is derived from sensory experience, and that there is no innate knowledge or ideas.
- **Argument from Environmental Ethics**: The argument that moral values should extend beyond human beings to include the natural environment and other non-human animals.
- **Argument from Ethical Egoism**: The argument that individuals should always act in their own self-interest, and that this is the ultimate standard of morality.
- **Argument from Feminist Ethics**: The argument that traditional ethical theories have been shaped by patriarchal values and assumptions, and that feminist ethics offers a more inclusive and just approach to moral decision-making.
- **Argument from Free Will**: The argument that free will is necessary for moral responsibility, and that the existence of evil is a consequence of free will. In other words, the existence of free will implies the existence of a non-physical aspect of reality, and that this is evidence for the existence of God.
- **Argument from Ignorance**: Assuming that something is true simply because it has not been proven false, or

vice versa. *"I don't know how the universe was created, so God must have done it."*

- **Argument from Induction**: The argument that knowledge claims based on induction (i.e., generalizations from empirical observations) are justified, despite the problem of induction.
- **Argument from Inference to the Best Explanation**: The argument that the best explanation for a given phenomenon is the one that best accounts for the available evidence.
- **Argument from Intuition**: The argument that some knowledge is self-evident or intuitively obvious, and that we can rely on our intuitions to guide our beliefs.
- **Argument from Miracles**: The argument that miracles provide evidence for the existence of God.
- **Argument from Moral Realism**: The argument that moral values and duties are objective and exist independently of human opinion or convention.
- **Argument from Moral Skepticism**: The argument that moral values and duties are subjective and do not exist independently of human opinion or convention.
- **Argument from Morality**: The argument that objective moral values and duties exist, and that these can only be explained by the existence of God.
- **Argument from Ontological Existence**: The argument that the concept of God as the greatest possible being necessitates his existence.
- **Argument from Pascal's Wager**: The argument that it is rational to believe in God, because the potential benefits of belief (eternal life) outweigh the potential costs of disbelief.
- **Argument from Personal Experience**: The argument that personal experiences provide evidence for the truth of a belief or claim.
- **Argument from Rationalism**: The argument that some knowledge is innate or a priori, and that reason alone can provide knowledge of necessary truths.

- **Argument from Reason**: The argument that the existence of reason and rationality imply the existence of a rational creator.
- **Argument from Relativism**: The argument that all truth claims are relative to culture, language, or historical context, and that there are no objective or universal truths.
- **Argument from Religious Experience**: The argument that religious experiences provide evidence for the existence of God.
- **Argument from Silence**: Assuming that the lack of evidence for something is evidence that it does not exist or is not true. *"There's no evidence that God exists, so God must not exist."*
- **Argument from Skepticism**: The argument that we cannot be certain of anything beyond our own perceptions and mental states, and that all knowledge claims are inherently uncertain.
- **Argument from Solipsism**: The argument that we cannot be certain of anything except our own consciousness, and that the existence of other minds and the external world can only be inferred.
- **Argument from the Impossibility of Infinite Regress**: The argument that an infinite regress of causes is impossible, and that this implies the existence of a first cause.
- **Argument from the Laws of Nature**: The argument that the laws of nature imply the existence of a lawgiver.
- **Argument from the Origin of the Universe**: The argument that the Big Bang implies the existence of a creator.
- **Argument from the Problem of Evil**: The argument that the existence of evil is incompatible with the existence of an all-powerful and all-good God.

- **Argument from Utilitarianism**: The argument that the morality of an action is determined by its ability to maximize overall happiness or pleasure.
- **Argument from Virtue Ethics**: The argument that the morality of an action is determined by its conformity to the virtues or character traits of the agent.
- **Argumentum ad Populum**: Appealing to popular opinion or the majority rather than to evidence or reason. *"Everyone knows that aliens are real, so it must be true."*
- **Atomism**: A philosophical theory that holds that reality is ultimately composed of indivisible particles or atoms.
- **Axiology**: The branch of philosophy concerned with values, including ethical, aesthetic, and epistemic values.
- **Bandwagon Fallacy**: Assuming that something is true or good because it is popular or widely accepted. *"Everyone is buying the new iPhone, so it must be the best phone on the market."*
- **Begging the Question**: Assuming that a conclusion is true in the premise of the argument. *"God exists because the Bible says so, and the Bible must be true because it was written by God"* or *"I am a good person because I always do good things."*
- **Behaviorism**: A psychological theory that emphasizes the importance of observable behavior and environmental stimuli in shaping human behavior and this is without reference to internal mental states.
- **Black or White Fallacy**: Assuming that only two options exist, when in reality there are more. *"You're either for us or against us."*
- **Burden of Proof**: Shifting the burden of proof from the person making a claim to the person who questions it. *"You can't prove that ghosts don't exist, so they must be real."*

- **Categorical imperative**: A moral principle put forth by Immanuel Kant that states one should always act in a way that could be made into a universal law.
- **Causal Determinism**: The belief that every event is caused by a prior event, and that all events follow a chain of causation.
- **Causation**: The relationship between an event or action (the cause) and a subsequent event or action (the effect), or the process by which one event brings about another.
- **Cherry-Picking**: Selectively presenting evidence that supports one's argument while ignoring evidence that contradicts it. *"The weather has been unusually cold this winter, so that proves that global warming isn't real."*
- **Circular Reasoning**: Using the conclusion of an argument as a premise. *"God exists because the Bible says so, and the Bible is the word of God."*
- **Cogito, ergo sum**: Latin for *"I think, therefore I am."* This is a famous statement made by philosopher Rene Descartes, which he used to prove the existence of the self.
- **Cognitive Science**: The interdisciplinary study of the mind and its processes, including perception, attention, memory, and decision-making.
- **Communism**: A political philosophy that advocates for the collective ownership of the means of production and the establishment of a classless society.
- **Communitarianism**: The belief that individual identity is shaped by the community and its values, and that moral and ethical decisions must be made in the context of this community.
- **Composition Fallacy**: Assuming that something is true of the whole, based on the fact that it is true of some part of the whole. *"These individual cells are all healthy, so the entire organism must be healthy."*

- **Composition/Division**: Assuming that what is true of a part is also true of the whole, or vice versa. *"The engine of this car is high-quality, so the whole car must be high-quality"* or *"This team is the best in the league, so all of the players on the team must be the best"* or *"Each brick in the wall is small and light, so the entire wall must be small and light."*
- **Consequentialism**: A moral theory that evaluates the rightness or wrongness of an action based on its consequences or outcomes.
- **Constructivism**: The belief that knowledge is constructed by individuals through interaction with the world, and that reality is therefore socially constructed.
- **Cosmological Argument**: The argument that the existence of the universe requires an explanation, and that this explanation is God.
- **Cosmopolitanism**: The belief that all human beings have equal moral worth, regardless of nationality or other social distinctions, and that individuals have a responsibility to promote the well-being of all people.
- **Critical Race Theory**: The body of work that examines the intersection of race and power in society, and seeks to understand and address racial inequalities and oppression.
- **Cultural Relativism**: The belief that moral and ethical values are relative to the culture in which they are held, and that there is no objective standard of right or wrong.
- **Dasein**: refers to the fundamental mode of being-in-the-world, characterized by self-awareness and a sense of temporal existence.
- **Deconstruction**: A method of literary analysis and philosophical inquiry that seeks to reveal and subvert the underlying assumptions and binary oppositions of a text or discourse. In other words, this philosophical method analyzes texts and language in order to

uncover the underlying assumptions and contradictions within them.

- **Deductive reasoning**: a method of reasoning in which a conclusion follows logically from the premises.
- **Deontology**: A moral theory that emphasizes the importance of following moral rules and duties, regardless of their consequences.
- **Determinism**: The belief that all events, including human actions, are ultimately determined by prior causes and conditions, and that free will is an illusion.
- **Dialectic**: A method of arguments, counterarguments, or discussions that involves the exchange of opposing viewpoints in order to arrive at a more comprehensive understanding of a concept or issue.
- **Dialectical materialism**: A Marxist theory that views historical and social change as the result of contradictions and conflicts between opposing social classes.
- **Division Fallacy**: Assuming that something is true of a part, based on the fact that it is true of the whole. *"The company as a whole is profitable, so all of its departments must be profitable."*
- **Dualism**: A philosophical theory that holds that reality is ultimately composed of two distinct or different things or substances in the world, such as mind and body.
- **Egoism**: A moral theory that holds that individuals should act in their own self-interest, even if this conflicts with the interests of others.
- **Empathy**: The ability to understand and share the feelings of another person.
- **Empirical**: Based on observation or experience, rather than on theory or speculation.
- **Empiricism**: A philosophical tradition that emphasizes the importance of experience and observation in gaining knowledge, or knowledge that comes primarily from sensory experience and observation.

- **Environmental Ethics**: The branch of ethics that examines the moral and ethical implications of human interactions with the natural world, and seeks to promote sustainable and responsible environmental practices.
- **Epistemological skepticism**: The philosophical position that knowledge is uncertain and that we cannot be certain of anything.
- **Epistemology**: The branch of philosophy concerned with the nature, sources, and limits of knowledge.
- **Equivocation**: Using a term with multiple meanings, and switching between them to make an argument appear stronger. *"I'm going to the bank to deposit some fish."*
- **Ethics**: The branch of philosophy concerned with moral principles and values, and their application to human behavior.
- **Eudaimonia**: A Greek term meaning *"happiness"* or *"flourishing,"* often used in discussions of virtue ethics.
- **Ex post facto rationalization**: this is the act of creating a rational explanation for a decision or action after the fact in order to justify it.
- **Existence precedes essence**: A concept used in existentialist philosophy to describe the idea that individuals create their own meaning and purpose in life through their actions and choices.
- **Existential angst**: A feeling of anxiety, dread, or despair that arises from the realization of the fundamental uncertainty and meaninglessness of human existence.
- **Existential nihilism**: the belief that life is inherently meaningless and devoid of objective purpose or values. Manipulators may use this to undermine others' beliefs, instill a sense of hopelessness, and justify their destructive actions.
- **Existentialism**: A philosophical and literary movement that emphasizes the individual experience of freedom,

choice, and responsibility in a meaningless or absurd world. This includes one's search for meaning in life.

- **False Equivalence**: False equivalence is a logical fallacy that occurs when two or more things are unjustifiably compared or equated, implying they are equal or similar when they are not. This fallacy disregards the differences in evidence, facts, and relevance between the arguments being presented. It can mislead by creating a false sense of balance or fairness and manipulate opinions by treating unequal ideas as if they hold the same value. False equivalence is commonly used in rhetoric, debates, and media to confuse audiences. An example is comparing the dangers of smoking cigarettes to the risks of eating fast food, where the magnitude and evidence of harm differ significantly. It is important to recognize false equivalence and critically evaluate information by considering evidence, context, and relevant factors to form an informed judgment.
- **Fallacious**: In philosophy, this refers to an argument or reasoning that is flawed or erroneous. Fallacies are common errors in reasoning that can mislead people into accepting a conclusion that is not supported by evidence or logical analysis.
- **Fallacy**: Dismissing an argument simply because it contains a fallacy. *"You used the appeal to authority fallacy, so your argument is invalid."*
- **Fallacy of Sunk Costs**: This fallacy is the argument that something should be continued because of the investment that has already been made in it, despite new evidence that it is not working. *"We can't abandon this project now; we've already invested too much time and money in it."*
- **False Analogy**: Comparing two things that are not actually similar in relevant ways. *"Banning assault weapons is like banning all guns. It's a violation of our Second Amendment rights,"* or *"Cars are like houses,*

so we should regulate them the same way we regulate houses," or "Banning assault rifles is like banning knives, because both can be used to kill people," or "The government is like a parent, and just like parents need to discipline their children, the government needs to discipline its citizens."

- **False Authority**: Citing an authority figure who is not an expert in the relevant field. *"My dentist said I should vote for this candidate, so I will."*
- **False Balance**: Giving equal weight to two sides of an argument, even when one side has overwhelming evidence in its favor. *"Some scientists say climate change is real, but others disagree."*
- **False Cause**: Assuming that because one event follows another, the first event must have caused the second. *"I wore my lucky socks and my team won the game, so my lucky socks must have caused the win,"* or *"I took an aspirin and my headache went away, so the aspirin must have cured my headache,"* or *"I prayed for it to rain, and then it rained, so my prayer caused the rain."*
- **False Consensus**: Assuming that everyone shares your beliefs or values. *"Everyone knows that God exists, why do you even bother questioning it?"*
- **False Dichotomy**: Assuming that there are only two possible options when there may be other possibilities. *"Either we go to war or we let them attack us first,"* or *"You're either with us or against us,"* or *"Either you love America or you hate America".*
- **False Dilemma**: Assuming that there are only two options, when in reality there may be many more. *"You're either with us or against us,"* or *"Either we build a wall, or we let in all the criminals".*
- **False Equivalence**: Comparing two things that are not actually comparable in a relevant way. *"Banning smoking in public places is just like banning freedom of speech,"* or *"People who drink coffee are just as bad*

as people who smoke cigarettes!" or *"Being a vegetarian is just like being a Nazi."*

- **False Precedent**: Arguing that because something has been done in the past, it should continue to be done in the future, regardless of changing circumstances or new information. *"We've always had slavery, so we should keep having it."*
- **Fatalism**: The belief that events are predetermined and inevitable, and that individuals have no control over their fate.
- **Feminism**: A social, political, and philosophical movement that advocates for gender equality and the dismantling of patriarchy. This states that efforts should be made to address and eliminate them.
- **Feminist Theory**: The body of work that seeks to understand and address gender-based inequalities and oppression, and promote gender equality and social justice.
- **Functionalism**: The theory that everything in the world can be explained by its function or purpose, rather than its material or physical properties.
- **Gambler's Fallacy**: Assuming that because something hasn't happened in a while, it is more likely to happen in the future. *"I've flipped heads three times in a row, so the next flip must be tail,"* or *"I lost the last 10 hands of poker, so I'm bound to win the next one."*
- **Gaslighting:** a manipulative tactic where individuals distort or deny reality to make their victims doubt their own perceptions, memories, and sanity. By sowing seeds of doubt, manipulators gain control and undermine their victims' confidence.
- **Genetic Fallacy**: Dismissing an argument based on its source or origin. *"I don't trust anything that comes from the mainstream media,"* or *"I can't take that argument seriously, it came from a conspiracy theory website,"* or *"I don't believe in evolution because it was proposed*

by an atheist," or *"You can't trust that news source, it's run by liberals."*

- **Global Justice**: The body of work that examines the moral and ethical implications of global inequalities and injustices, and seeks to promote social justice and equality on a global scale.
- **Hasty Generalization**: Drawing a broad conclusion based on insufficient evidence. *"I met one rude person from New York, so everyone from New York must be rude."*
- **Hegelian dialectic**: A philosophical method that involves the synthesis of opposing viewpoints or ideas in order to arrive at a higher level of understanding.
- **Hegelianism**: The philosophical system developed by Georg Wilhelm Friedrich Hegel, which emphasizes the dialectical process of history and the ultimate reconciliation of opposing forces.
- **Hegemony**: The dominance of one social group or ideology over others, often achieved through cultural or political power.
- **Hindsight bias**: a cognitive bias that refers to the tendency to believe, after an event has occurred, that one would have predicted or expected the outcome beforehand.
- **Humanism**: A philosophical and ethical stances that emphasizes the importance of human values, dignity, culture, and freedom, and rejects supernatural or religious beliefs.
- **Ideal observer theory**: A moral theory that evaluates the rightness or wrongness of an action based on how it would be judged by an ideal observer who is fully informed and impartial.
- **Idealism**: A philosophical theory that emphasizes the importance of the mind or consciousness in understanding reality. This is the view that reality is ultimately mental or spiritual in nature, rather than material or physical.

- **Intellectual arrogance**: Manipulators may employ a superior intellectual façade, using their knowledge and intellect to belittle others, dismiss opposing viewpoints, and establish themselves as the ultimate authority.
- **Intentionality**: The property of mental states or processes that involves being "about" or directed toward an object or content.
- **Jungianism**: While not a standalone philosophy, I am including this term here because it was used to attack me. The concept refers to the approach developed by psychologist Carl Jung, which highlights the importance of the unconscious mind and its impact on human behavior. It suggests that psychological problems arise from conflicts among different aspects of the psyche and seeks to explore and integrate these conflicts through methods such as dream analysis. The goal of a Jungian therapist is to help individuals achieve greater wholeness and psychological well-being by increasing their awareness of unconscious conflicts.
- **Loaded Language**: Using emotionally charged words or phrases to influence someone's opinion. *"Illegal aliens are flooding our country and stealing our jobs."*
- **Loaded Question**: Asking a question that assumes a certain answer. *"Why do you hate America?"* or *"Have you stopped beating your wife?"*
- **Logic**: The branch of philosophy concerned with reasoning and argumentation.
- **Logical fallacy**: am umbrella term that covers many others listed such as *ad hominem, straw man, red herring, appeal to antiquity,* and *false equivalence.*
- **Logical positivism**: A philosophical movement that emphasizes the importance of empirical evidence and scientific verification in the evaluation of truth claims.
- **Logos**: A Greek term used by philosophers to refer to the fundamental principles of order and knowledge that govern the universe.

- **Marxism**: The social and economic theory that emphasizes the importance of class struggle and the ultimate replacement of capitalism with socialism or communism.
- **Material dialectics**: A concept used in Marxist philosophy to describe the way in which material conditions and contradictions give rise to social change and historical progress.
- **Materialism**: A philosophical theory that emphasizes the importance of material objects and physical processes in understanding reality.
- **Metaphysics**: The branch of philosophy concerned with the nature of reality and existence.
- **Middle Ground Fallacy**: Assuming that the correct answer must be somewhere between two extremes, without considering the possibility that one extreme might be correct. *"Some people say we should ban all guns, while others say we should allow anyone to have any gun they want. The correct answer must be somewhere in the middle."*
- **Middle Ground Fallacy**: Assuming that the middle ground between two extreme positions is always the best course of action. *"Since one group wants to abolish the death penalty and another group wants to expand it, we should just keep it as is."* Or *"Some people think we should abolish all guns, while others think we should have no restrictions at all. I think we should meet in the middle and have some reasonable regulations,"* or, *"The Republicans say we need to cut taxes, and the Democrats say we need to raise taxes, so we should compromise and keep taxes the same."*
- **Moral Argument**: The argument that objective moral values and duties exist, and that these can only be explained by the existence of God.
- **Moral Relativism**: The belief that moral judgements and principles are subjective and vary from person to person or culture to culture. This allows manipulators

to justify their immoral actions by claiming that morality is a matter of personal opinion.

- **Moving the Goalposts**: Changing the criteria for a successful argument after the argument has been made, in order to avoid being proven wrong. *"I said that I would believe in climate change if the temperature rose by 2 degrees,"* or *"Okay, so maybe my theory doesn't explain everything yet, but I'm sure we'll find evidence for it eventually."*
- **Natural law**: A moral or legal theory that holds that there are inherent principles or values that believes that certain moral principles are inherent in the natural world. These principles govern human behavior and can be discovered through reason.
- **Naturalism**: The belief that everything in the world can be explained by natural causes, without the need for supernatural explanations.
- **Naturalistic Fallacy**: Assuming that what is natural is inherently good or right. Example: "Humans are meant to eat meat, so it's morally justified to kill animals for food."
- **Nietzschean perspectivism**: Drawing from Friedrich Nietzsche's philosophy, this tactic suggests that there are no objective truths and that all perspectives are equally valid. Manipulators may exploit this notion to evade accountability and assert their own distorted version of reality.
- **Nihilism**: A philosophical position that holds that life has no inherent meaning or value. The rejection of all religious, moral, and philosophical beliefs, often accompanied by a sense of despair or pessimism.
- **Nirvana Fallacy**: Rejecting a solution or proposal because it is not perfect or does not completely solve the problem. *"I know this bill will reduce pollution. It won't eliminate it fully, so I'm voting against it."*
- **No True Scotsman**: Dismissing counterexamples to a claim by redefining the term in an ad hoc way. *"No true*

Scotsman would put sugar in their porridge. Oh, you put sugar in your porridge? Well, then you're not a true Scotsman. " Re-defining a term in order to exclude cases that contradict a claim such as *"No true Christian would support abortion,"* or *"No true Christian would support same-sex marriage."*

- **Non-Sequitur**: A conclusion that does not logically follow from the premises. *"All dogs are mammals. Therefore, all mammals are dogs."*
- **Noumenon**: A concept used in Kantian philosophy to refer to the thing-in-itself, which exists independently of our perception or experience of it.
- **Objectivism**: A moral or philosophical theory that holds that there are objective moral or epistemological truths that can be discovered through reason or observation.
- **Objectivity**: The quality of being impartial, unbiased, or free from personal opinions or feelings.
- **Ontological Argument**: The argument that the existence of God can be proved by reason alone, based on the concept of God as the most perfect being.
- **Ontology**: The branch of philosophy concerned with the nature of being and existence.
- **Pascal's Wager**: The argument that it is rational to believe in God, even in the absence of conclusive evidence, because the potential rewards of belief are so great.
- **Personal Incredulity**: Rejecting an argument or claim because it's difficult to understand or because it goes against your personal beliefs. *"I can't believe that humans evolved from apes. It just seems too ridiculous,"* or *"I can't believe in evolution, it's too complicated."*
- **Phenomenology of perception**: A philosophical theory developed by Maurice Merleau-Ponty that emphasizes the embodied and situated nature of

human perception. It's a philosophical approach that emphasizes the subjective experience of consciousness and perception.

- **Phenomenon**: A concept used in Kantian philosophy to refer to the way in which things appear or are perceived by the mind.
- **Platonism**: The philosophical system developed by Plato, which emphasizes the existence of eternal, unchanging Forms or Ideas that underlie the material world.
- **Poisoning the Well**: Discrediting someone before they even have a chance to make their argument. *"I don't know why you would listen to anything John has to say, he's a known liar."*
- **Positivism**: A philosophical and scientific tradition that emphasizes the importance of empirical observation and verifiable evidence in gaining knowledge instead of using intuition or speculation.
- **Post Hoc Ergo Propter Hoc**: Assuming that because one event followed another, the first event caused the second. *"I wore my lucky socks to the game and we won, so my socks must have helped us win."*
- **Postcolonial Theory**: The body of work that examines the legacy of colonialism and imperialism, and seeks to understand and address the power imbalances and inequalities that continue to exist between former colonizing and colonized societies.
- **Postcolonialism**: A critical theory and intellectual movement that explores the cultural and political effects of colonialism and imperialism.
- **Postmodernism**: A philosophical and cultural movement that emphasizes the relativity, subjectivity, and instability of knowledge and meaning. This includes the importance of language and social construction.

- **Pragmatism**: A philosophical approach that emphasizes practical consequences of beliefs and ideas as well as the usefulness in solving problems.
- **Primitivism**: A belief in the superiority or desirability of primitive or traditional lifestyles, often accompanied by a rejection of modern technology and civilization.
- **Principle of sufficient reason**: The philosophical principle that holds that everything must have a sufficient reason or explanation for its existence or occurrence.
- **Problem of Evil**: The argument that the existence of evil and suffering in the world is incompatible with the existence of an all-powerful, all-knowing, and all-good God.
- **Queer Theory**: The body of work that challenges traditional binary notions of gender and sexuality, and seeks to understand and address the complexities and diversity of human experience in these areas.
- **Rationalism**: A philosophical tradition that emphasizes the importance of reason and logical analysis in gaining knowledge. This is a view that knowledge can be obtained through reason and intuition, rather than sensory experience.
- **Rationality**: The quality of being logical, reasonable, and justifiable.
- **Realism**: a theory that holds that reality exists independently of our perception or experience of it.
- **Red Herring**: Bringing up an irrelevant topic to divert attention from the original issue. *"I know I lied about my qualifications, but what about all the good things I've done for the company?"* or *"I know I cheated on my taxes, but what about all those politicians who cheat on their spouses?"* or *"We need to focus on gun control, not mental health issues,"* or *"I know I didn't do my homework, but my dog is sick and needs to go to the vet,"* or *"We need to focus on the economy, not on climate change."*

- **Reductionism**: The belief that complex phenomena can be explained by reducing them to their component parts, and that all explanations ultimately reduce to fundamental scientific principles.
- **Relativism**: The philosophical position that holds that knowledge, truth, or morality are not absolute but rather depend on the particular cultural or historical context, culture, or perspective of the individual or group with no objective or universal standards.
- **Skepticism**: A philosophical approach that questions the possibility of knowledge, truth, or certainty. This position holds that it is impossible to know anything with certainty.
- **Slippery Definition**: Using vague or ambiguous language to make an argument that is difficult to pin down or refute. *"Love is just a feeling, you can't really define it."*
- **Slippery Slope**: Arguing that a small action will inevitably lead to a much larger, negative outcome without sufficient evidence. *"If we let gay people get married, then soon people will be marrying their pets,"* or *"If we legalize marijuana, next thing you know everyone will be doing heroin and society will crumble."*
- **Social contract theory**: A political theory that attempts to explain the origins and nature of the state, and the relationship between individuals and their government. The theory holds that individuals give up some of their individual rights and freedoms to a government in exchange for protection and security. This social contract is based on the idea of mutual obligation and consent, where both the government and the governed agree to certain terms and obligations.
- **Solipsism**: A philosophical position that holds that the self is the only thing that can be known or verified to exist.

- **Sophistry**: the art of using clever and deceptive arguments to manipulate and deceive others, often by exploiting logical fallacies and rhetorical techniques.
- **Special Pleading**: Making an exception for a particular case without providing sufficient justification. *"I know I said lying is always wrong, but it's okay in this case because I didn't want to hurt her feelings."*
- **Straw Man**: Misrepresenting an opponent's argument in order to make it easier to attack. *"My opponent wants to take away your freedom by banning guns,"* or *"My opponent wants to take away our guns and leave us defenseless against criminals,"* or *"The Democrats want open borders, which means they want to let in all the criminals and terrorists,"* or *"You're saying we should just let people do whatever they want? That's a recipe for anarchy!"* or *"My opponent wants to take away your freedom and control your life,"* or, *"My opponent thinks that we should have no restrictions on guns. That's a ridiculous position."*
- **Structural-functionalism**: A sociological theory that emphasizes the interrelatedness and interdependence of social institutions and their functions in maintaining social order.
- **Structuralism**: A method of analysis that seeks to uncover the underlying structures and patterns that shape language, culture, and society.
- **Sympathetic magic**: This concept, rooted in anthropology and occult practices, explores the belief that objects or actions resembling each other can influence or interact with one another. It suggests that by imitating or manipulating one object or action, a desired effect can be achieved on another object or action connected to it through a symbolic or sympathetic link. It revolves around the idea that there is a connection between similar or related things, often expressed as "like produces like." Sympathetic magic is found in diverse cultural and spiritual traditions,

involving rituals, symbols, and gestures aimed at utilizing this perceived connection to manifest desired outcomes.

- **Teleological Argument**: The argument that the complexity and order of the universe imply the existence of a designer or creator.
- **Teleology**: The philosophical study of purpose, goals, or ends in nature or human affairs... the purpose or design in nature.
- **Texas Sharpshooter Fallacy**: Cherry-picking data in order to find patterns that fit a preconceived notion. *"My horoscope said I would have a good day, and I did, so horoscopes must be true."* or *"Look at all these studies that show my diet plan works! Oh, those other studies that show it doesn't work? They're just outliers."* Or *"I know that eating vegetables is bad for me because the last time I ate a vegetable, I got sick."* This fallacy is the selective use of data or evidence to support a position while ignoring contradictory data or evidence. *"The stock market is up, so our economic policies must be working."* Or *"Look at these data points that support my argument, and ignore all the ones that contradict it."*
- **Transcendence**: The ability to rise above or go beyond ordinary experience, often associated with spiritual or mystical experiences.
- **Tu Quoque**: Accusing someone of hypocrisy in order to avoid addressing their argument. *"You can't criticize my drinking; you drink just as much as I do!"* Attempting to defend your own wrongdoing by pointing out the wrongdoing of others. *"Why are you criticizing me for cheating on me when you cheat on me all the time?"* or *"You can't criticize me for cheating on my taxes when you cheated on your diet."* Basically, not following your own advice, such as *"You say we should recycle, but you don't recycle yourself,"* or *"You

can't say smoking is bad for my health when you smoke too."

- **Universalism**: The belief in the existence of universal principles or values that apply to all people and cultures.
- **Utilitarianism**: A moral theory that emphasizes the importance of maximizing overall happiness or pleasure in making moral decisions. This theory evaluates the rightness or wrongness of an action based on its ability to maximize overall happiness or pleasure for the greatest number of people.
- **Virtue ethics**: A moral theory that emphasizes the development of virtuous character traits, such as courage, honesty, and compassion, as the basis for ethical decision-making.
- **Zeitgeist**: A German term meaning "spirit of the times," often used to describe the cultural, intellectual, and social climate of a particular historical period.
- **Zen**: A Buddhist philosophy that emphasizes the importance of achieving enlightenment. This is a philosophical and religious tradition originating in China and Japan, which emphasizes the cultivation of mindfulness, meditation, and non-attachment to achieve enlightenment.
- **Zeno's paradoxes**: A series of paradoxes presented by the Greek philosopher Zeno of Elea, which challenge the possibility of motion and change by demonstrating the inherent contradictions in our understanding of space, time, and infinity.

The given list covers several tactics, but it's not exhaustive. Therefore, it's essential to familiarize yourself with these tactics to remain vigilant. They are frequently employed to deceive, manipulate, and harm others for personal gain or ideological reasons (Nocera et al, 2020). The aggressive and harmful behaviors exhibited by monsters and creeps can have detrimental effects on various aspects of their victims' lives. These behaviors, characterized by hate, spite, unethical conduct, and often illegal actions, can hinder the victim's ability to support their families and result in missed opportunities (Garcia et al, 2021).

On the following graphic, it is my opinion that YouTube has not removed videos related to harassment very often. This lack of action might explain the substantial increase in incidents of harassment on their platform.

Distribution of videos removed from YouTube worldwide from 2nd quarter 2019 to 2nd quarter 2022, by reason

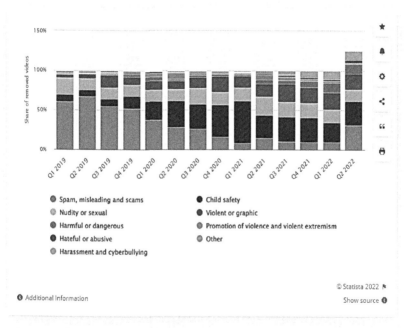

(*www.statista.com/statistics/1132956/share-removed-youtube-videos-worldwide-by-reason*)

Next, we will explore the common personality traits frequently observed in monsters and creeps. It is crucial to acknowledge that not all individuals exhibiting these traits are involved in cyber-hatred. Nevertheless, we can observe recurring patterns that indicate similarities in their personality traits, as supported by research findings per Johnson (2020), Smith (2018), and Brown et al. (2019). In simpler terms, similar to how handwriting analysis can reveal distinct patterns that reflect the personality traits of individuals, specific behavioral patterns can also be observed in other contexts. These patterns indicate common characteristics displayed by individuals who hold specific personality traits.

"Oh, look, it's just another friendly monster spreading love and joy through cyber-hatred. How original!"

(sarcasm fully intended)

Thoughts & Insights:

Thoughts & Insights:

Unveiling the Psyche of Social Media Monsters & Creeps with Keyboards

While monsters and creeps may vary in their intentions, tactics, and goals, they do exhibit certain shared personality traits, such as:

- **Manipulative tactics**: he employs various strategies, such as deception, lying, or flattery, to manipulate and exploit others for personal gain.
- **Exploitative relationships**: he tends to use and take advantage of others without genuine care or concern for their well-being.
- **Lack of empathy**: he demonstrates an inability or unwillingness to understand or share the emotions and perspectives of others.
- **Arrogance and grandiosity**: he displays an exaggerated sense of self-importance and superiority, often seeking admiration and attention.
- **Superficial charm**: he is highly skilled at presenting himself in a charming and charismatic manner, using it as a tool for manipulation.
- **Impulsivity and risk-taking**: he engages in impulsive behaviors and takes risks without considering the potential consequences.
- **Lack of accountability**: he often evades responsibility for his actions, blaming others or external factors for his own mistakes or shortcomings.
- **Aggression and hostility**: he exhibits aggressive tendencies, both verbally and physically, as a means to control or intimidate others.
- **Lack of long-term commitments**: due to his self-centered nature and disregard for others, he struggles with maintaining long-term relationships, commitments, or stable employment.

- **Machiavellian mindset**: he adopts a strategic and manipulative mindset, seeking power, control, and personal gain through calculated means.
- **Emotional detachment**: he appears emotionally detached or shallow, lacking genuine emotional connections and often only displaying emotions for manipulation purposes.
- **Sexual promiscuity**: he engages in casual sexual encounters without emotional attachment or consideration for the well-being of their partners.
- **Boundary violations**: he disregards personal boundaries and social norms, invading others' privacy or personal space to satisfy his own needs.
- **Lack of remorse or guilt**: he shows little to no remorse for his harmful actions, often rationalizing or justifying his behavior instead.
- **Glibness and superficiality**: he engages in shallow conversations, avoiding emotional discussions and vulnerability or uses big words to sound intelligent or educated as a way to earn respect by intellectual intimidation.
- **Deception and lying**: he frequently engages in dishonesty, manipulation, and deceptive practices to achieve his personal objectives.
- **Lack of close friendships**: he struggles to maintain genuine friendships; people initially like him but are soon repelled.

While possessing these traits does not necessarily indicate someone will become a cyber-hater, they can collectively contribute to the intricate and manipulative nature often found in such individuals.

But that's not all.

Within the Dark Triad, the constructs are: **narcissism, psychopathy,** and **Machiavellianism**. However, I am going to also include **sociopathy** and **anti-social** in this section because I believe it is fitting in the context and for the mission of this book.

Understanding these terms allows us to better comprehend the motivations and behaviors exhibited by individuals who can be described as monsters or creeps. The Dark Triad traits are often associated with such behaviors. Psychopathy, which involves manipulation and a lack of empathy, can contribute to intentionally causing harm to others online. Sociopathy, characterized by a disregard for societal norms and the rights of others, can result in a lack of empathy and a willingness to engage in harmful activities. Antisocial behavior, particularly in individuals diagnosed with Anti-Social Personality Disorder, encompasses various traits that contribute to their involvement in online aggression and bullying (Jones, 2015).

Different personality traits influence individuals' online tendencies, motivations, and engagement in harmful activities (Lewis, 2014). When the three categories of the Dark Triad are combined, they create a toxic environment where harmful online behaviors flourish due to a disregard for social norms (Zajenkowski et al., 2018).

Thoughts & Insights:

Narcissists

Individuals who struggle with mental disorders such as depression or anxiety often experience a loss of self-confidence and find it challenging to present themselves positively within their community. This vulnerability makes them more susceptible to social media addiction as a means to boost their ego. They create an idealized self-image and consistently seek validation from virtual friends. When engaging in negative behaviors online, they are often driven by a sense of self-importance, and a desire to promote themselves or their agenda (Winter, 2015).

Understanding narcissism requires acknowledging that a formal diagnosis of Narcissistic Personality Disorder (NPD) should only be made by a qualified mental health professional after a thorough evaluation of the individual's unique symptoms and behaviors. However, we can explore common traits and behaviors associated with narcissism, recognizing that different types of narcissists exist, each with their own distinct behavioral patterns.

Narcissists, in general, display an inflated sense of self-importance. They prioritize their own desires and interests over others, often lacking empathy and disregarding the well-being of those around them. This self-centered mindset often drives their engagement in harmful online behavior, disregarding the impact on others.

Moreover, narcissistic individuals tend to be quite arrogant, often display a sense of entitlement and superiority, and harbor envy toward others. They also tend to overestimate their own significance, intelligence, and abilities. When they don't receive the desired validation from others, they may react with emotional volatility, showing signs of irritability, anger, and insecurity.

Their self-centered attitude prioritizes their own needs above everyone else's, as they strive to avoid feelings of vulnerability, worthlessness, or inadequacy.

Upon reviewing the "Evidence" section of this book, it is highly likely that you will come across the presence of many of these characteristics in individuals whom I often refer to as haters, monsters, and creeps.

Here are the 10 common types of narcissists:

- **Antagonistic Narcissist**: he is highly competitive and places significant emphasis on rivalry. He frequently engages in disagreements and arguments with others, seemingly driven by a desire to prove himself superior. He has a tendency to exploit or take advantage of others for personal gain. Additionally, he experiences difficulty in forgiving others and struggles with issues of trust, making it challenging for him to establish or maintain trusting relationships.
- **Cerebral (Intellectual) Narcissist**: he derives self-importance from his intellect and considers himself clever and more intelligent than others. He may try to make others feel unintelligent to feed his ego.
- **Communal Narcissist**: despite his claims of possessing a strong moral code, he consistently acts in contradiction to his professed beliefs. While he may exhibit signs of overt narcissism, he also demonstrates a heightened sensitivity to situations he perceives as unfair. Paradoxically, he views himself as generous or saintly, often expressing emotional outrage in response to circumstances he deems unjust. However, his actions do not align with the thoughts or beliefs he professes, revealing a notable inconsistency in his behavior.
- **Controlling Narcissist**: he exhibits a strong desire for control and dominance over others, using

manipulation, intimidation, or coercion to maintain power and authority.

- **Covert Narcissist**: he appears shy or introverted but harbors a deep need for attention and admiration. They may use passive-aggressive tactics to control and manipulate others.
- **Entitled Narcissist**: he firmly holds the belief that he is entitled to receive special treatment, privileges, and resources, displaying a complete disregard for the needs and rights of others.
- **Exhibitionist Narcissist**: he seeks attention and validation near constantly by engaging in flamboyant or attention-seeking behaviors. He often relies on his physical appearance or accomplishments to garner admiration from others
- **Grandiose Narcissist**: he exhibits dominant and outgoing behavior, placing himself at the center of attention. He displays self-centeredness and an intense drive to outperform others in a competitive manner. Observable indications of these traits include a strong desire for praise and attention, a high level of self-esteem, an inflated perception of his abilities, a tendency to assert dominance in interpersonal interactions, a lack of empathy and insensitivity towards others' needs, an arrogant demeanor, a sense of entitlement, and a preoccupation with himself.
- **Malignant Narcissist**: the most severe type, his behavior combines narcissistic and antisocial traits. This combination is regarded as a serious condition that significantly affects interpersonal relationships within both the family and society. Signs of this severe type include paranoia, aggression, sadism, vindictiveness, an extreme intolerance for criticism, and a deep fear of others mocking or belittling them.
- **Online Narcissist**: he uses online platforms as a means to garner attention, validation, and admiration. He often presents an idealized version of himself,

carefully curating his online persona. However, he also often engages in harmful behaviors such as online harassment or cyberbullying, using the anonymity and distance provided by the digital realm to harm others.

- **Overt Narcissist**: he possesses an exaggerated sense of self-importance and constantly craves admiration and attention from others. He openly exhibits a grandiose self-image, frequently boasting about his achievements, talents, or perceived superiority. Engaging in attention-seeking behaviors and seeking validation from external sources are common traits of his. He strongly desires to be acknowledged as special or unique. In conversations, he tends to dominate, disregarding the needs and emotions of others, displaying a lack of empathy. These self-centered behaviors and attitudes are readily evident to those around him, as he makes no effort to conceal or disguise them.

- **Parasitic Narcissist**: he exploits and takes advantage of others for personal gain, often using charm and manipulation to manipulate his victims.

- **Sexual Narcissist**: he excessively idolizes his own sexual prowess and employs manipulative tactics involving sex to control others. He may engage in serial cheating and demonstrate a proclivity for engaging in violent sexual acts. Sexual narcissism encompasses elements of somatic and cerebral narcissism (above) as well.

- **Somatic Narcissist**: he derives his self-worth from his physical appearance and often obsesses over it. This obsession can lead him to criticize the appearances of others while prioritizing his own needs and desires.

- **Spiritual Narcissist**: he manipulates his spirituality to rationalize harmful actions and presents an idealized version of himself. He utilizes spiritual language to intimidate others, appearing outwardly sensitive but with the underlying intention of asserting superiority over them.

- **Vulnerable Narcissist**: he possesses a fragile self-esteem and frequently adopts a victim mentality when confronted with his behavior. By assuming the role of the victim, he seeks reassurance and sympathy from others, attempting to deflect attention away from his actions and garner support for himself.

Please note that not all individuals with these traits will exhibit all of these behaviors; these are simply examples.

While it is possible for various types of narcissism to overlap, there is typically a dominant category that characterizes an individual's behavior. Nevertheless, narcissistic individuals commonly employ tactics such as stalking, slandering, discrediting, and sabotaging those whom they perceive as threats. They may launch smear campaigns and engage in character assassination, even if their targets are completely unaware of the narcissist's existence. These individuals perceive their targets as mortal enemies, harboring intense animosity towards them (Brown et al, 2019).

Even when the victim or target of the narcissist responds in a respectful, factual, and logical manner to the narcissist's aggression, he tends to twist the narrative to portray the victim as the aggressor. He may label the victim as unreasonable due to their defensive actions, regardless of the target's appropriate response (McCullough et al, 2003). This tactic is frequently employed by narcissists, and in my observation, it was quite evident as one of the strategies employed by my haters against me.

Two-Faced Art by Mozelle Martin
(www.VisualDiversity.art)

Psychopaths, Sociopaths, & Anti-Socials

While the terms "psychopath," "sociopath," and "antisocial" are often used interchangeably, they do have distinct meanings. Here is an explanation to clarify their differences:

- **Psychopath**: is typically associated with individuals who exhibit a specific set of personality traits and behaviors characterized by a lack of empathy, remorse, and conscience. Psychopathy is often viewed as an inherent personality disorder rooted in biological and genetic factors.

- **Sociopath**: is used to describe individuals who display antisocial behaviors, disregard for social norms, and a disregard for the rights and well-being of others. Sociopathy is often believed to develop as a result of environmental factors, such as childhood experiences or upbringing.

- **Antisocial**: is a broad term that refers to individuals who exhibit a persistent pattern of disregard for and violation of the rights of others. This term is often used in the context of Antisocial Personality Disorder (ASPD), which is a diagnosable mental disorder characterized by a lack of empathy and a disregard for societal norms.

It's important to note that these terms may have slightly different meanings and interpretations depending on the context and the professional field using them.

We will examine the six anti-social types soon, but for now...

Here are 14 common types of psychopaths:

- **Antisocial Psychopath**: he engages in criminal behavior and violates the rights of others. He shows impulsiveness and aggression while disregarding social norms.
- **Charming Psychopath**: he is highly skilled at manipulating others, using charm to gain trust.
- **Corporate Psychopath**: he operates in the corporate world, employing charm and manipulation to climb the ladder, often at the expense of others.
- **Covert Psychopath**: he is skilled at concealing his psychopathic traits and behaviors, often appearing normal to others.
- **Cult Leader Psychopath**: he leads a cult or extremist group, manipulating followers using fear tactics or promises of enlightenment.
- **Histrionic Psychopath**: he is highly dramatic and seeks attention and admiration from others. He uses charm and manipulation to fulfill his needs.
- **Malignant Psychopath**: he is considered very dangerous; he engages in acts of extreme violence or cruelty.
- **Narcissistic Psychopath**: he displays an inflated sense of self-importance, lacks empathy, and manipulates others to fulfill his personal desires. He may become angry or vindictive if his needs are not met.
- **Primary Psychopath**: he exhibits several psychopathic traits from an early age, often before age 15. He engages in impulsive or aggressive behaviors and lacks empathy, remorse, or guilt.
- **Sadistic Psychopath**: he takes pleasure in causing pain or suffering to others, often engaging in acts of cruelty or violence for personal enjoyment.

- **Secondary Psychopath**: he develops most psychopathic traits later in life, usually as a result of perceived trauma.
- **Sexual Psychopath**: he has sexual desires for non-consensual or taboo activities, often involving force, coercion, or violence.
- **Successful Psychopath**: he achieves high levels of success in his professional and/or personal life but engages in unethical or immoral behavior behind the scenes to attain goals.
- **White-Collar Psychopath**: he works in a white-collar profession such as business or finance, is often involved in embezzlement, fraud, or other financial wrongdoings.

Please note that not all individuals with these traits will exhibit all of these behaviors; these are simply examples.

In summary, the term sociopathy is used to describe individuals with antisocial behavior, while the diagnosis of Antisocial Personality Disorder (ASPD) provides a more specific framework for understanding individuals with chronic patterns of antisocial behavior. ASPD encompasses a clinical diagnosis with defined criteria, whereas sociopathy is a broader term without specific diagnostic criteria (Brown, 2018).

Regardless of the terminology, individuals with sociopathic and antisocial tendencies exhibit a distinct set of characteristics. They display high levels of impulsivity and seek sensory stimulation. Their attitudes are often irresponsible and grandiose, with a self-centered focus. Their emotional responses tend to be superficial, making it difficult to easily identify them as perpetrators. They are skilled in deception and show little remorse or guilt.

Furthermore, these individuals score low on measures of anxiety, fear, and empathy (Nguyen et al., 2022). They have a disregard for societal norms, rules, and the rights of others. Manipulative and exploitative behaviors are common. Their mindset revolves around personal gain and can manifest in activities aimed at causing distress to their targets.

Their desire for control and power over others, combined with their propensity for violence, often leads to criminal behaviors. They derive satisfaction from creating chaos and frequently expose the flaws of others, employing negative social media posts and language patterns that fuel their impulsivity and recklessness. Their online presence often emanates an atmosphere of violence, death, and anger.

"Oh, look at me, I'm the master of the digital domain, spreading negativity and fear from behind my keyboard."

#CyberBullyExtraordinaire   (sarcasm fully intended)

Sociopaths

Recognizing the distinctions between psychopathy, sociopathy, and antisocial behavior is essential when examining their connection to cyberhatred. By understanding these differences, we can gain valuable insight into the potential motivations, thought processes, and behaviors of individuals characterized as haters, monsters, and creeps. This deeper understanding empowers us to develop more precise interventions and preventive measures that specifically target the issue of cyber-hatred.

Here are the 10 common types of sociopaths:

- **Manipulative Sociopath**: he is highly skilled at manipulating and exploiting others for personal gain. He may use charm, deception, and other tactics to control others and use them to his advantage.
- **Aggressive Sociopath**: he displays aggressive tendencies, both verbally and physically. He may use intimidation, and violence as tools to exert dominance over others.
- **Charismatic Sociopath**: he has a captivating personality. He is adept at presenting himself in an engaging and charismatic manner, which can be used to manipulate and deceive others.
- **Impulsive Sociopath**: he exhibits impulsive and reckless behaviors, disregarding the potential consequences. Rules and societal norms hold little weight for him.
- **Antisocial Sociopath**: he has a blatant disregard for social norms, rules, and the rights of others. He may engage in criminal activities, violate laws, and show little remorse for his actions.

- **Parasitic Sociopath**: he manipulates and exploits others for his own benefit without any genuine concern for the well-being of those he harms. He may rely on others for financial support, emotional resources, or other forms to acquire personal gain.
- **Disorganized Sociopath**: he often displays chaotic and unpredictable behavior. He may struggle with maintaining stability in his life, have difficulty forming long-term plans, and exhibit erratic patterns of behavior.
- **Narcissistic Sociopath**: he has an inflated sense of self-importance, a lack of empathy, and a willingness to exploit and manipulate others to fulfill his desires.
- **Exploitative Sociopath**: he takes advantage of others without genuine care or concern for their well-being. He may use people as a means to achieve his goals and discard them when they no longer serve his needs.
- **Emotionally Detached Sociopath**: he is emotionally detached and exhibits shallow emotions. He has difficulty empathizing with others and may manipulate emotions solely for his own benefit.

To summarize, psychopathy and sociopathy are both personality disorders characterized by antisocial behavior and a disregard for the rights and feelings of others. Psychopathy is generally considered a more severe and innate condition, while sociopathy is thought to be influenced by environmental factors and upbringing.

Psychopaths often display a lack of empathy, shallow emotions, and manipulative behaviors. In contrast, sociopaths may have a stronger emotional connection but still demonstrate significant antisocial tendencies.

When it comes to social media trolling and bullying (cyber-hatred), both psychopaths and sociopaths can engage in these behaviors, but their motivations and approaches differ.

Psychopaths tend to employ calculated tactics, manipulation, and leverage the relative anonymity of the internet to exert power over others. By engaging in deviant behaviors, they aim to cause emotional distress to their targets.

Sociopaths, on the other hand, may act impulsively, driven by personal grievances, a lack of regard for social norms, and a desire to provoke reactions. While they may also derive pleasure from causing distress, their behavior is often more reactive and less premeditated compared to psychopaths.

It's important to note that not all individuals with psychopathic or sociopathic tendencies will engage in cyber-hatred. The presence of Dark Triad traits does increase the likelihood of such behavior, but it does not guarantee that every individual with these traits will exhibit problematic online conduct.

Other factors, such as personal circumstances, history, and environmental influences, also play a role in determining whether someone with these traits will engage in cyber-hatred or similar behaviors.

Thoughts & Insights:

Anti-Socials

As mentioned earlier, the term "antisocial" is indeed broad and can encompass various behaviors and attitudes. However, in a clinical context, when referring to individuals with antisocial tendencies, it commonly indicates Antisocial Personality Disorder (ASPD).

Here are 6 common types of anti-social individuals:

- **Exploitative**: he consistently exploits and manipulates others for personal gain, disregarding the well-being and rights of those around him. He engages in deception, cheating, and using others as a means to meet his own needs without consideration for their welfare.
- **Reckless**: he engages in impulsive and risky behaviors, often disregarding the potential consequences that may arise. This includes a lack of concern for his own safety and the safety of others, which can lead to dangerous situations.
- **Dissocial:** he consistently displays a disregard for social norms and rules, often engaging in behaviors that are considered deviant or even criminal. These may include acts of theft, vandalism, or aggression, among others.
- **Secondary:** his behavior is often influenced by external factors, such as substance abuse or a negative environment. These factors can contribute to the manifestation of impulsive and aggressive behaviors. It is important to note that these behaviors may stem from underlying issues rather than inherent personality traits.
- **Covetous**: he harbors a strong desire for what others possess and is willing to resort to theft or manipulation in order to acquire those belongings. He feels entitled

to the possessions of others and demonstrates little remorse for his actions.

- **Reputation-defending**: his primary focus lies in safeguarding his own reputation. To achieve this, he may resort to aggressive or manipulative behaviors, aiming to maintain a positive image or evade negative consequences. Tactics like spreading rumors or undermining others are often employed to protect his own interests.

In summary, individuals may display a combination of traits from different categories of antisocial types, emphasizing that these categories are not mutually exclusive. It is essential to differentiate between casually labeling someone with these tendencies and formally diagnosing them with Antisocial Personality Disorder (ASPD).

While these categories aid in understanding antisocial behavior, a comprehensive evaluation is necessary to determine if an individual meets the diagnostic criteria for ASPD.

Art by Mozelle Martin
(www.VisualDiversity.art)

Thoughts & Insights:

Machiavellians

Machiavellians derive their name from Niccolò Machiavelli due to their tendencies to engage in manipulative and duplicitous behaviors for personal gain. They hold the belief that manipulation is crucial for achieving success and employ tactics like lies, flattery, and strategic maneuvering. Despite displaying charismatic leadership qualities, they are prone to betraying others and engaging in deceitful actions. Interestingly, Machiavellians also have a fear of social rejection and often prefer online relationships that provide greater opportunities for manipulation.

Individuals within the Dark Triad exhibit unique characteristics but share a proficiency in manipulating others. They exploit social services and government agencies, and when denied assistance, they assume the role of victims to deceive others. This manipulation tactic aligns with the actions of my haters, as evident in the provided evidence section.

To illustrate this phenomenon, I can share a personal example. I was once acquainted with someone who willingly placed her toddler son in a children's home. However, on the same day, she manipulated the situation to appear on the evening news, falsely claiming that she was forced to give up her child due to a lack of government assistance. In reality, she had little interest in employment or parental responsibilities and did not require government programs as the child's grandmother provided significant monthly support for years.

In summary, Machiavellians possess the charm and social focus seen in narcissists, while also exhibiting the cynicism and disregard for ethics associated with psychopaths (Canaday, 2013).

Here are 16 common types of Machiavellians:

- **Academic Machiavellian**: he manipulates academic settings such as using others' research or ideas to advance his own career or goals.
- **Corporate Machiavellian**: he is skilled at manipulating others in a corporate setting, often using charm and manipulation to climb the corporate ladder.
- **Criminal Machiavellian**: he engages in criminal activities, such as fraud, theft, or organized crime.
- **Cyber Machiavellian**: he manipulates online situations and relationships, often engaging in cyber-hatred.
- **Financial Machiavellian**: he gains a financial advantage through fraudulent or unethical means.
- **Manipulative Machiavellian**: he is highly skilled at manipulating others to get what he wants, often using charm and flattery.
- **Narcissistic Machiavellian**: he has an inflated sense of self-importance and may use his tendencies to achieve personal gain and control over others.
- **Political Machiavellian**: he is skilled at manipulating political situations and relationships to achieve his goals, often using deceit to gain power or influence.
- **Power-Hungry Machiavellian**: he seeks power and control over others, and uses any number of tactics to achieve his goals.
- **Sadistic Machiavellian**: he enjoys causing pain or suffering to others and uses tactics to control or manipulate his victims.
- **Sexual Machiavellian**: he uses his tendencies to achieve sexual gratification or to manipulate sexual partners.
- **Sexual Manipulator Machiavellian**: he uses his tendencies to manipulate and exploit sexual partners, often engaging in sexual coercion.

- **Social Machiavellian**: he is skilled at manipulating social situations to his advantage, often using charm to gain influence and control over others.
- **Strategic Machiavellian**: he uses his manipulative traits to develop and execute strategic plans, prioritizing his own goals over the well-being of others.
- **Vengeful Machiavellian**: he uses his tendencies to seek revenge or retaliate against others who he feels have wronged him, often using manipulation or deception to achieve his goals.
- **Workplace Machiavellian**: he uses his manipulative traits to control situations and relationships in the workplace, often using deceit to gain power or influence.

No matter which of these categories, if you are *unfortunate* enough to live with someone on this triad...

- When you try to instill order, he will create chaos.
- When you set boundaries, he will push against them until the boundary breaks.
- When you say "no", he will force hell upon you until you say "yes".

When sharing your experiences with others, you might encounter surprising reactions. It is common for people to dismiss your claims as a "lovers' quarrel" or a "misunderstanding." Some individuals may even blame you or suggest that you are overreacting.

While this response can be frustrating and invalidating, it is important not to immediately hold the naysayers or disbelievers accountable. It is likely that they have never encountered a situation like yours, making the details you describe seem to bizarre for real life.

Just when you thought the Dark Triad was bad enough, here comes the Dark Tetrad.

The Dark Tetrad takes the already troubling Dark Triad and introduces another disturbing trait: *sadism*. In addition to narcissism, Machiavellianism, and psychopathy, individuals with the Dark Tetrad also derive pleasure and satisfaction from inflicting pain and suffering onto others as a means of exerting dominance (Jones, 2015).

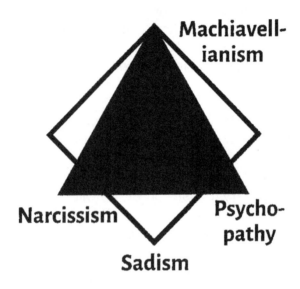

Schadenfreude, characterized by intentionally causing harm to others and taking pleasure in their suffering, can provide insight into the motivations behind cyber-hatred. Individuals exhibiting schadenfreude in the context of cyber-hatred derive satisfaction from causing distress to their targets and may disregard the negative impact on others (Smith, 2010).

Trolling behavior is often driven by schadenfreude, with individuals perceiving it as enriching their own online experience rather than hindering it (Brubaker et al., 2021). The dark tetrad trait of sadism is closely associated with aggression and online trolling (Johnson, 2020; Thompson et al., 2017).

Cyber-hatred encompasses various forms of harmful online behavior, including cyber-bullying, cyber-harassment, and cyber-stalking (Davis & Jones, 2016). Research indicates that dark triad and tetrad traits (D-traits), specifically sadism and psychopathy, are significant predictors of cyber-hatred (Martin et al., 2021). These traits serve as coping mechanisms and sources of power, entertainment, or relief for individuals engaging in cyber-hatred (Nocera, 2020; Du et al., 2018).

The motivation behind cyber-hatred can also stem from a fear of missing out on victims' online activities or a desire for constant surveillance (Kircaburun et al., 2022). These dynamics provide insights for developing strategies to prevent and mitigate the impact of cyber-hatred.

Furthermore, research suggests that cyber-haters may target individuals they perceive as more successful as a means of compensating for their own real-life inadequacies (Kircaburun et al., 2022). This serves as a reminder of what they have not achieved themselves.

Understanding the gender differences in cyber-hatred is also important. Men are more likely to engage in cyberbullying and trolling, while women tend to exhibit higher levels of cyber-stalking (Smith & Johnson, 2017). Men also demonstrate higher levels of antisocial personality traits, which are considered precursors to engaging in cyber-hatred behaviors (Szabo et al., 2019). Women, on the other hand, may exhibit higher levels of social media addictions characterized by increased social interactions and lower antisocial tendencies (Brown & Williams, 2019).

Overall, comprehending the psychological factors underlying cyber-hatred and its association with D-traits provides valuable insights into the possible motivations and behaviors of individuals involved. These insights inform the development of interventions and preventive measures to target cyber-hatred and foster healthier online environments.

"Behind every monstrous cyberbully lurks an expert in cowardly keystrokes and hateful tactics!"

#OnlineMonster #KeyboardWarrior

(sarcasm fully intended)

Correlation of D-Traits and Social Media

The combination of Dark Triad and Tetrad traits (D-Traits) has been extensively researched and shown to be correlated with chronic social media use and internet addiction (Nguyen et al., 2022). Problematic internet use (PIU) is associated with negative outcomes such as depression, anxiety, stress, loneliness, and physiological dysfunction, with adolescents and emerging adults being particularly susceptible due to their high internet usage (Lee et al., 2020; Sampasa-Kanyinga et al., 2019).

Certain personality traits, including higher neuroticism, lower extraversion, lower conscientiousness, lower openness to experience, and lower agreeableness, have been linked to PIU (Kardefelt-Winther, 2017). Understanding the correlation between D-Traits and social media usage can help form interventions and strategies aimed at promoting responsible online behavior while mitigating negative consequences (Kircaburun et al., 2022).

The prevalence of D-Traits on social media is a concerning aspect, with grandiose and vulnerable narcissism being commonly observed (Zajenkowski et al., 2018). Individuals exhibiting D-Traits manipulate social feedback on platforms to align with their goals (Twenge et al., 2010). Social media monsters and creeps exploit the platform to shame and bully others, disregarding different perspectives and hindering understanding (Bell et al., 2021). They may also feign victimhood when confronted by their actual victims (McCullough et al., 2003). *More on this in the "Evidence" section.*

The rise of D-Traits among millennials reflects a shift towards prioritizing money, image, and fame over community and self-acceptance (Twenge, 2014).

Facebook's influence on social media and D-Traits is noteworthy, but let's not forget that personality traits are largely shaped before joining any platform (Twenge et al, 2010).

Interventions should focus on education, empathy-building, ethical use of social media, and providing resources for emotional well-being to address these issues. Promoting healthier online interactions and creating a positive digital environment can help mitigate the negative consequences associated with D-Traits on both the Dark Triad and Dark Tetrad (Bell et al., 2021).

However, it is crucial to recognize that correlation does not imply causation when examining the relationship between D-Traits and social media engagement. Individual differences within these trait categories should be acknowledged, and factors such as personal values, upbringing, self-regulation skills, and social support networks also play significant roles in determining online behavior.

Art by Mozelle Martin
(www.VisualDiversity.art)

Thoughts & Insights:

Case Studies

While I won't delve into the personal stories of the courageous individuals listed below, I find it essential to acknowledge and respect their experiences. By doing so, we come to understand that cyber-hatred can affect anyone. If you wish to learn more about these individuals, I recommend conducting an online search and reaching out to them directly for additional information. At this moment, my intention is to simply recognize their stories as a way to honor and celebrate their remarkable resilience.

- **Aaron von Ehlinger**: has taken legal action against various political figures who were involved in a campaign of harassment and intimidation towards him. The lawsuit claims that these individuals targeted him as a form of retaliation for his refusal to step down from his position in the Idaho Legislature.
- **Alisha Marie**: has spoken out about this issue and her own struggles with anxiety and panic attacks.
- **Alyssa Milano**: has been the target of online harassment and cyberbullying, particularly related to her political views and advocacy.
- **Amanda Todd**: took her own life at the age of 15 after experiencing years of cyberbullying. Prior to doing so, she had shared her story in a YouTube video in which she described how a stranger had convinced her to flash her breasts on webcam when she was 12 years old. He then used the image to blackmail and harass her online and offline. During the book's launch on July 23, 2023, I featured her story on my YouTube channel. Subsequently, it was shared with Amanda's family.
- **Amber Rose**: has been the target of online harassment and cyberbullying, particularly related to her personal life and relationships.

- **Andie Case**: has discussed the impact this problem has on mental health and shares her own experiences on the topic.
- **Ashley Judd**: has spoken publicly about her experience with online harassment and cyberbullying.
- **Bella Hadid**: has been the target of online harassment and cyberbullying, particularly related to her personal life and relationships.
- **Bella Thorne**: has shared her experience with online harassment and cyberbullying, particularly related to her personal life and relationships.
- **Blind creator**: has vision problems in which his haters used DoorDash to deliver glasses and eyedrops as a way to mock his blindness. As he stated, *"they are the epitome of what they speak against."*
- **Carlos Mencia**: has been the target of criticism and controversy throughout his career, including accusations of plagiarism and insensitive humor.
- **Caroline Flack**: was the target of online cyber-hatred, particularly related to her personal life and relationships, until her 2020 death.
- **Caroline Hirons**: has spoken publicly about her experience with online harassment and cyberbullying, particularly related to her criticism of the beauty industry.
- **Chrissy Teigen**: has been the target of online harassment and cyberbullying, particularly on Twitter.
- **Criminologist colleague of mine**: who I have known since the late 1990s, had a similar situation. She endured bullying and stalking from a cyber-mob that not only trashed her books on Amazon but also created a website filled with slanderous lies and hateful content. To make matters worse, other creators stole her work and posted her videos on their own channels. She took action by filing a copyright infringement complaint with YouTube, which initially

took down the stolen videos. However, to her dismay, YouTube reinstated them after 10 days, causing the haters to gloat and label her a liar based on this "proof." Although she fought back, she realized that the process was burdensome and time-consuming, leading her to understand that it wasn't the right approach for her. Despite enduring all of this, she remains on the platform, although other channels continue to attack and defame her.

- **David Diga Hernandez**: at last minute I included this one because yesterday, while casually passing by the food court at the local mall, I overheard a video playing where someone was discussing how their name and photos were being used to create fake accounts, which were then used to randomly email people and solicit donations. Intrigued, I was immediately compelled to discover the identity of this person. So, I discreetly observed the food court during the bustling Saturday afternoon until I located the individual responsible for playing the video. To my surprise, I discovered that the person sharing their experience was an evangelist minister, author, and television host. The video in question was titled *"Holy Spirit Loves to See This, but Few Christians Do It"* and was recorded on May 24, 2023. I encourage you to watch the video yourself, as he provides details of his personal encounter with cyber-hatred.
- **Demi Lovato**: has spoken publicly about her experience with cyberbullying, particularly related to her struggles with mental health and addiction.
- **Detective colleague of mine**: although he didn't want to be mentioned in this book, I could write a full chapter on his experiences. If you follow true crime, you likely already know his story.
- **Dove Cameron**: has been the target of online harassment and cyberbullying, particularly related to her personal life and relationships.

- **Dr. Holly Jacobs**: back in 2011, intimate images of her were shared online without her consent, causing them to be distributed among her employer, peers, friends, family members, and even strangers. This distressing incident resulted in harassment and severe damage to her mental health. As a consequence, she faced the loss of educational and professional opportunities as well as strained relationships. Seeking justice, she turned to the authorities and legal counsel, but unfortunately received minimal support and assistance. In response to this lack of aid, she took matters into her own hands and initiated a grassroots movement called *"End Revenge Porn."* Through this initiative, she aims to provide support and assistance to victims and survivors of similar ordeals.
- **Dr. Simon Goddek**: has a PhD in biotechnology and is a scientific writer who was called a pseudoscientist and corona denier, banned from social media for sharing his research, and much more.
- **Emma Jenkins**: has worked with a variety of organizations to help inspire and empower individuals to reach their goals. She was viciously targeted because of her Christian faith.
- **Euleen Castro**: was viciously targeted because of her weight.
- **Eva Gutowski**: has spoken out about her own experiences with cyberbullying and has used her platform to raise awareness. She urges her viewers to be upstanders.
- **Jameela Alia Burton**: has been the target of online harassment and cyberbullying, particularly related to her advocacy for social justice and mental health awareness.
- **Jameela Jamil**: has been the target of online harassment and cyberbullying, particularly related to her advocacy for body positivity and mental health awareness.

- **Jameela Razzaq**: has been the target of online harassment and cyberbullying, particularly related to her conservative religious views.
- **Jennifer Olaleye**: has spoken out about her experience and advocated for awareness, focusing on the impact that cyber-hatred has on mental health. She also highlighted the need for social media platforms to uphold their terms of service while sharing her own experiences.
- **Jesse & Alyssa from Pure Living for Life**: were targeted, harassed, stalked, and so much more. I can't even begin to explain what they went through.
- **Jessica Valenti**: was the target of online harassment and cyberbullying, particularly related to her advocacy for women's rights.
- **JS**: If you're familiar with the Summer Wells case, you might be aware of the unjustified hostility that has been directed towards JS. Regrettably, despite being unaware of this specific case, I found myself unintentionally analyzing JS's handwriting (then unknown to me). I publicly shared a video on my channel for less than a day, and it was only afterwards that I realized what had occurred. As soon as I became aware of the issue, I promptly removed the non-identifying video from my channel and released an equally non-identifying apology video. Unfortunately, my original video was later circulated on another YouTube channel through auto-generated transcripts. I want to emphasize that I strongly condemn any form of bullying and harassment, as I would never engage in such behavior towards anyone. Many have considered JS a suspect in the case. Regardless, I sincerely apologize to JS for any direct or indirect harm caused by the short-lived presence of my video.
- **Kathy Griffin**: was the target of online harassment and cyberbullying, particularly related to her political views and activism.

- **Kelly Marie Tran**: was the target of online harassment and cyberbullying, particularly related to her role in the Star Wars franchise.
- **Kesha**: was the target of online harassment and cyberbullying, particularly related to her legal battle with music producer Dr. Luke.
- **Lady Gaga**: was the target of online harassment and cyberbullying, particularly related to her political views and advocacy.
- **Lena Dunham**: was the target of online harassment and cyberbullying, particularly related to her political views and activism.
- **Lena Headey**: has spoken publicly about her experience with online harassment and cyberbullying, particularly related to her role in the Game of Thrones franchise.
- **Leslie Grace**: has spoken publicly about her experience with cyberbullying and online hatred.
- **Leslie Jones**: was the target of a coordinated online harassment campaign in 2016, resulting in the temporary suspension of her Twitter account.
- **Lindsay Lohan**: was the target of online harassment and cyberbullying, particularly related to her personal life and relationships.
- **Lisa-Michelle Kuchartz**: became the target of relentless harassment and cyberstalking, but instead of succumbing to fear, she decided to fight back and achieved a historic victory in an international legal case. Today, she actively shares her personal experiences and the valuable lessons she learned while navigating the intricacies of law enforcement and the judicial system. Witnessing the alarming rise in youth suicide and self-harm resulting from cyberbullying, she has devoted herself to advocacy for prevention. Collaborating with legislators and fellow advocates, she works tirelessly to evaluate existing

laws and propose effective measures to combat online abuse, both for young individuals and adults. Her dedication lies in creating a safer digital environment for all.

- **Lizzo**: has been the target of online harassment and cyberbullying, particularly related to her body positivity message and activism.
- **Mary Elizabeth Winstead**: was the victim of a cyberattack in 2014 that resulted in the theft and public release of personal photos.
- **Megan Fox**: has spoken publicly about her experience with online harassment and cyberbullying, particularly related to her appearance and personal life.
- **Megan Meier**: took her own life in 2006 at the age of 13 after being cyberbullied by a group of teens, including an adult neighbor, who created a fake MySpace profile to befriend her and then turned on her with hurtful messages and comments.
- **Meredith Foster**: discusses the negative impact cyberbullying can have on mental health. She shares stories of other content creators who have been affected by online harassment. She emphasized the importance of standing up against online hate and negativity.
- **Mia Stammer**: has spoken out about cyberbullying and promotes positivity and self-love. She has been a strong advocate for mental health awareness and shared her own struggles with anxiety and depression.
- **Miley Cyrus**: was the target of online harassment and cyberbullying, particularly related to her personal life and relationships.
- **Millie Bobby Brown**: was the target of online harassment and cyberbullying, particularly related to her appearance and personal life.

- **Monica Lewinsky**: became a victim of cyberbullying and public shaming after her affair with President Bill Clinton was exposed in 1998.
- **Paris Hilton**: was the victim of a cyberattack in 2005 that resulted in the theft and public release of personal photos and information.
- **Phoebe Prince**: ended his life in in 2010 due to the cyberbullying when he was a teenager.
- **Rebecca Black**: was the subject of widespread online bullying and harassment after the release of her viral song "Friday" in 2011.
- **Rebel Wilson**: became a victim of cyberbullying, enduring relentless online harassment and criticism throughout her career. The attacks she faced targeted various aspects of her life, including personal jabs at her appearance, weight, and talent. Despite the adversity she faced, she managed to develop effective coping mechanisms to deal with the onslaught of cyberhate. Drawing strength from her experiences, she transformed into an advocate against cyberbullying. Through her advocacy work, she raises awareness about the damaging effects of online harassment and shares her personal journey of resilience and self-empowerment.
- **Rosie O'Donnell**: was the target of online harassment and cyberbullying, particularly related to her political views and activism.
- **Ryan Halligan**: ended his life in 2003; he was a teenager.
- **Sarah Silverman**: was the target of online harassment and cyberbullying, particularly related to her political views and activism.
- **Shay Mitchell**: has spoken publicly about her experience with cyberbullying and online hatred.

- **Sofia Richie**: has been the target of online harassment, particularly related to her personal life and relationships.
- **Tanya Burr**: has spoken publicly about her experience with cyberbullying and online hatred.
- **Tyler Clementi**: ended his life in 2010 while in college due to being harassed and publicly exposed because of his sexual orientation.
- **Zendaya**: was the target of online harassment and cyberbullying, particularly related to her appearance and racial identity.

The seriousness of cyber-hatred is illustrated by various examples in this list, spanning different age groups and professional backgrounds. While some of the names of individuals are anonymous, their identities can be revealed promptly if required by law.

For those interested in exploring more stories, the following names can serve as a helpful starting point: *August Ames, Jadin Bell, Danny Chen, Goo Hara, Hana Kimura, Tyler Long, Haruma Miura, Hamed Nastoh, Brodie Panlock, Rahtaeh Parsons, Audrie Pott, Nicola Ann Raphael, Jamey Rodemeyer, Rebecca Ann Sedwik, Ty Smalley, Choi Jin-ri (Sulli), Tyrone Unsworth, Sladjana Vidovic, Kenneth Weishuhn, Dawn Marie Wesley, Kelly Yeomans, Dolly Everett, DIYfferent,* and *Harry Lew.*

Engaging in online activities exposes individuals to the possibility of encountering malicious individuals ("monsters") or those who invade others' privacy ("creeps with keyboards"). Although precise statistics regarding cyberbullying incidents targeting *adult professionals* are not readily available, numerous studies and surveys shed light on the increasing prevalence of such incidents.

According to a 2019 survey conducted by Pew Research Center, 18% of adults in the United States reported experiencing online harassment, including name-calling, attempts at shaming or embarrassing, and physical threats. Among those reporting harassment, 41% experienced severe forms such as stalking or physical threats.

A 2021 report by Ditch the Label, an anti-bullying charity based in the UK, revealed that 44% of surveyed adults encountered cyberbullying, with 41% of incidents occurring on social media platforms.

This represents a significant increase in just two years. Extrapolating this trend, it is estimated that the current figure is closer to 66% (Davis, 2022), although, as you already know, 79% of cyber-hatred occurs on YouTube.

While instances of YouTube creators attempting to kill another creator are rare, it has occurred at least once (Grizzly True Crime, 2022).

Nonetheless, harm inflicted on the internet remains a significant issue, and the following three examples serve as a mere sampling of YouTube creators who have encountered legal challenges, underscoring that there are indeed consequences for such actions.

• **Jake Paul**: confronted legal issues related to his behavior and actions. Lawsuits have been filed against him, alleging assault, negligence, and other claims.
• **Tana Mongeau**: She has faced lawsuits arising from the failure of her convention, "TanaCon," which led attendees to pursue legal action for various concerns.
• **Ray William Johnson**: confronted a copyright infringement lawsuit concerning the usage of a viral video

on his channel. Eventually, the lawsuit was resolved through an out-of-court settlement.

In addition, one notable case that warrants exploration is the story of James Jackson, also known as Gregory James Daniel, who gained fame through his online persona "Onision." With a substantial following on platforms like YouTube, Onision has been at the center of considerable attention and controversy. Beginning in 2019 and persisting to the present day, he has been involved in a series of legal problems and controversies.

Multiple individuals, including former partners, have come forward with allegations of misconduct, manipulation, and emotional abuse against him. These accusations have sparked substantial scrutiny and generated significant backlash within online communities. It is important to note that these allegations have not only affected his online reputation but have also resulted in legal actions and investigations.

The case of James Jackson, or Onision, serves as a prominent example highlighting the power and impact of online personalities and the serious consequences that can arise from allegations of misconduct within the digital realm. It demonstrates the need for thorough examination and discussion of the ethical boundaries and responsibilities of individuals who possess significant online influence.

Art by Mozelle Martin
(www.VisualDiversity.art)

Cyber-Hatred Pandemic

The term "cyber-hatred pandemic" is not currently defined in academic or professional contexts. However, it is evident that incidents of cyber-hated and other types of online harassment have been on the rise in recent years, paralleling the increased influence of the internet and social media in our daily lives.

Cyber-hatred is a societal issue rooted in human behavior, whereas a pandemic primarily refers to the spread of infectious diseases. Nevertheless, there are some similarities in how they manifest and spread, making it the perfect metaphor.

- Like a pandemic, cyberhatred can spread across different regions and affect individuals worldwide. The internet and social media platforms have a global reach, allowing hateful content to reach diverse audiences and transcend physical boundaries.
- Just as a contagious disease rapidly spreads from person to person, cyberhatred can quickly propagate online. Hateful messages, offensive comments, and discriminatory content can be disseminated rapidly through social media, online forums, and other digital platforms.
- Similar to a pandemic affecting a significant number of individuals, cyberhatred has become increasingly prevalent. Numerous people have experienced or witnessed online harassment, hate speech, and discriminatory behavior, highlighting the widespread nature of this issue.
- Both cyberhatred and pandemics can have detrimental effects on individuals and society as a whole. Online hate can cause emotional and physical distress, affect financial well-being and can even lead to real-world consequences such as violence. Similarly, pandemics

can result in severe illness, loss of life, economic disruptions, and strain on healthcare systems.

- Addressing cyberhatred, like combating a pandemic, requires collaborative efforts. It necessitates individuals, communities, organizations, and online platforms coming together to promote tolerance, respect, and digital well-being. Similar to how public health measures and interventions are implemented during a pandemic, strategies such as awareness campaigns, education, and stronger policies can help mitigate cyberhatred.

The online realm provides anonymity and distance, making cyber-hatred a pervasive issue among adult professionals. Furthermore, the presence of hate speech and extremist content on social media platforms is concerning as it can facilitate the spread of hateful ideologies and potentially incite violence (Cikanavicius, 2019).

Acknowledging the reality of cyber-hatred and online harassment is essential, requiring collaborative efforts to establish a safer and more respectful online environment. This entails educational initiatives that raise awareness about the impact of such behaviors (Clarkson, 2021).

However, it is unfortunate that there is currently limited hope for immediate change in terms of platforms adopting and enforcing more stringent policies and regulations to effectively combat cyber-hatred and online harassment.

"Congratulations, cyberhaters! Your keyboard courage has earned you a spot in the Hall of Pathetic Internet Warriors. Keep spreading the love... or rather, the hatred."

(sarcasm fully intended)

Thoughts & Insights:

Boundaries

After my experience and the decision to write this book, I embarked on an extensive *public* investigation into the individuals who have been my most vocal critics. Now, let me make it crystal clear: I had no interest in delving into their *personal* lives as that is not my concern. My sole focus was on their *public personas*, using only Google as my investigative tool.

In my quest to gather evidence for my book, I wanted to uncover whether the monsters or creeps who had hastily criticized me with their biased and hateful content were actually guilty of their own hypocrisy.

As you will soon find out, they definitely were.

It's important to note that I have never engaged in any form of malicious or criminal behavior like that of my haters, nor will I ever do so.

In other words, I have never and will never create any hate-filled videos or any other content, online or offline, to call them out by their real names, usernames, or any other identifying method.

Instead, I wrote this book with the belief that readers like you have the intelligence and skills to identify these individuals through independent research should you choose to do so. In fact, they may be channels you follow but we'll delve deeper into that topic later.

Now, let's look at the evidence of my story as I simultaneously expose their hypocrisy...

"Behold, the nocturnal genius who thrives on spreading darkness through their keyboard strokes! Beware mortals, for their vampiric creepiness knows no bounds!"

(sarcasm fully intended)

The Evidence

Initially, I was excited about the idea of incorporating video and audio links, as well as screenshots, into this book to provide evidence regarding the individuals being discussed. However, my federal lawyer strongly advised against it, citing the unethical behavior and lack of fairness and trustworthiness displayed by these individuals.

Instead, my legal team recommended including typed transcripts of the content, while ensuring the identities of those involved remain undisclosed. Following their guidance, this section of the book will primarily focus on presenting the statements made by the individuals referred to as "haters." Following each transcript, I will share my thoughts and responses.

By including these transcripts, my goal is to both educate and provide tangible evidence, or "receipts," that support the claims made throughout this book. This approach allows readers to gain a deeper understanding of the interactions and inner dynamics of this growing problem.

Please note that there may be some repetition in my responses as they are deliberately included to emphasize the point.

 **Buckle Up, Here we go...**

HATERS: "Mozelle engages in ex post facto rationalization, which I would like to see her employ before someone gets arrested, rather than after the fact. This behavior reflects confirmation bias, similar to the reliance on body language analysis, which lacks empirical support. Mozelle and the Behavioral Panel may be skilled in persuasive communication and storytelling, but their abilities to perform without any embellishments remain questionable."

- **My Thoughts**: This term refers to the process of creating a logical explanation retroactively to justify a decision or action, even if the original decision was impulsive or driven by emotions. This behavior often stems from a desire to avoid admitting that a decision was made for the wrong reasons or to evade taking responsibility for one's actions. While I cannot speak for the Behavioral Panel, for me, this is untrue. Firstly, my interactions have been limited to less than 1% of all the individuals I have analyzed throughout my 35-year international career. Secondly, there are videos on my YouTube channel that specifically debunk their claims.

HATERS: "A lot of people think graphology is legitimate but it's the same as psychics and astrology."

- **My Thoughts**: It is essential to differentiate graphology from fields such as psychics and astrology. In mental or physical health examinations, the diagnosis is typically based on the patient's reported symptoms. Psychologists and medical doctors, for instance, rely on prior knowledge directly provided by the patient to form their professional opinions. The haters consider their work "science-based". Contrary to the claims of the haters, when analyzing someone's handwriting, I intentionally do not want any prior information about the individual. Instead, my analysis is solely based on the characteristics and patterns present in the handwriting itself. This lack of prior knowledge is a crucial aspect of graphology, so it is ironic that the "monster mob" accuses my work of lacking scientific basis. While graphology may not be classified as a *hard* science, it is a specialized field that employs specific methodologies rooted in observable patterns and indicators. These methodologies allow for analysis and interpretation based on the unique characteristics present in the handwriting.

HATERS: "You need to approach a random person on the street and demonstrate your ability to predict with at least 80% accuracy whether they will commit a crime. If your prediction proves true when that person gets arrested and charged six months later, then you can consider your prediction successful."

- **My Thoughts**: I have conducted numerous instances of the work they mentioned, and they can find several video interviews with investigative professionals documenting these experiences on my YouTube channel. However, it is important to note that the showcased videos are not the only ones available, and I can provide evidence of these situations at any given time.

HATERS: "We are courageous enough to confront these malicious individuals and unethical channels, as they have a detrimental impact on the reputation and success of our high-quality channels. It is imperative for us to unite and urge YouTube to enforce their Terms of Service, ensuring a fair and ethical online environment."

- **My Thoughts**: If the platform exercised proper oversight and displayed even a small degree of empathy towards the victims, the haters would have their channels suspended due to their repeated and blatant violations of the Terms of Service. In some cases, these violations have persisted over a prolonged period of time.

HATERS: "If we are unable to persuade others through logical reasoning and factual evidence, resorting to shunning and ridicule becomes an alternative. When the animal kingdom utilizes this approach, the bad ones leave or are driven away. Our objective on this platform should be to achieve the same outcome by discouraging and marginalizing those who engage in negative behavior."

- **My Thoughts**: We are humans, not animals, and based on what I do know, the main victims they have attempted this with continue to have successful channels thereby raising doubt about the effectiveness of shunning and ridicule. It seems that the primary motivation behind these haters' channels may be centered around expanding their own viewership to generate clicks and profit from sensationalism, rather than upholding ethical principles and integrity.

HATERS: "I firmly believe that Mozelle and that detective are part of a criminal syndicate. He had his channel removed for cyberbullying before it was later reinstated by YouTube."

- **My Thoughts**: It is indeed intriguing that the actions attributed to the detective, which supposedly led to the removal of his channel, are precisely what these haters have been engaging in consistently for years, yet their channels remain unaffected. Regarding the notion of a criminal syndicate, I can only find amusement in - and feel pity toward - their desperate attempts to find any semblance of substance.

HATERS: *They said this about another creator...* "He is going to be on the internet forever and earn a livelihood by exposing innocent people without taking any responsibility for his actions."

- **My Thoughts**: Once again, it is clear that the haters fail to live up to the principles they espouse. They persistently participate in the exact behaviors they accuse others of, even when those accusations lack any foundation. Regrettably, it seems that presently there is no system in place to hold the haters responsible for their own actions on the platform. Hopefully, a change in this regard will occur sooner rather than later.

HATERS: "Mozelle lacks both ethics and professionalism and can be described as someone who indulges in unsubstantiated beliefs and practices, often referred to as woo-woo."

- **My Thoughts**: It is indeed intriguing that a video of me analyzing a convicted murderer has been present on their website(s) for over 20 years. Considering their perception of me, if they truly hold such a negative view of my skill, one might wonder why the video is still there. Plus, if they've known of me for 20 years, why weren't they hateful to me before I appeared on the detective's show in 2022?

HATERS: "While some may view our video as disrespectful towards Mozelle, we believe it is more disrespectful that she chooses to deceive the people who trust and believe in her."

- **My Thoughts**: Once again, it is worth noting that there are videos available on my channel that debunk their claims and expose their falsehoods. Again, without naming them or calling them out.

HATERS: "Her content on YouTube falls under the category of true crime pseudoscience. It is important to exercise caution when encountering such material, no matter how tempting it may be to believe the claims made about [criminal]."

- **My Thoughts**: Yet again, it is worth noting that there are videos available on my channel that debunk their claims and expose their bias.

HATERS: "It is so easy to prove these bad actors are liars and dangerous to society."

- **My Thoughts**: Again, it is indeed puzzling that these creators chose to feature me in a segment exposing psychics despite having my content on their platforms for decades. If they genuinely believed I was a fraud, one wonders why my content was initially allowed and why it continues to be available. In my opinion, there are a few possibilities: either these creators fear harassment from the same critics and join in as a self-protective measure, or they lack the ability to conduct independent research. Another option could be that they exhibit traits associated with the Dark Triad and / or Dark Tetrad personalities, or perhaps it's a combination of each.

Ironically, these haters accuse their victims of lacking independent research and critical thinking skills, which I find truly laughable. Perhaps they should consider pursuing a career in comedy.

Furthermore, they criticize YouTube for seemingly lacking compassion in taking action against channels and creators who consistently violate the platform's terms of service by engaging in harassment. In using their words, they must believe that all of their own hateful channels should be dealt with accordingly. I must admit, I agree. It would not be difficult to expose their deceptive tactics and falsehoods, as evidenced by the material I have at my disposal. Soon, you will realize just how skilled they are at speaking with hypocritical forked tongues.

HATERS: "Many supporters of these quack channels are right-wing hacks, religious zealots, and extremists. However, if we examine the teachings and actions of Jesus, it is likely that he would lean towards leftist principles. He would probably challenge and debunk conspiracy theories, as he was not one to place blind trust in established authorities. Jesus demonstrated care and compassion for the sick and marginalized, and he lived a life of poverty rather than pursuing material wealth."

- **My Thoughts**: I am certain that I am included in their assumption. However, it's worth noting that the derogatory categories these haters placed their victims into provides valuable insight into their own personalities. Using their example, one should then assume that all haters, monsters, and creeps are left-winged atheists, right? Although that would be completely unfair, many of my haters have repeatedly mocked Christians and admitted their anti-Christian beliefs. Yet, I have encountered individuals from across the political and religious spectrums during my career who do not engage in cyber-hatred and who are kind and compassionate.

HATERS: "I don't care if you like me but I am exposing who these bad actors really are and you just can't ignore the evidence. Once you start supporting them, you will deny any proof that you've been duped by them."

- **My Thoughts**: From the information provided, it appears that the haters are indirectly describing themselves and admitting to deceiving their viewers. In my opinion, if the viewers who possess critical thinking skills read this book and reflect on the negative comments they have heard from these haters or revisit their offensive content, they will likely recognize the hypocrisy displayed by these hateful individuals. Compassionate, intelligent, and logical viewers may come to realize that the haters they follow are not true to their claimed principles.

HATERS: "Smart people talk about ideas, mediocre people talk about events, simple-minded people talk about people. It might sound condescending and I don't care because it's true."

- **My Thoughts**: These haters have engaged in name-calling, persistently labeling their victims as *frauds, liars, charlatans, bad actors, tragedy pimps*, and more, for hours and even years. In using their own words, they have successfully proven themselves to be simple-minded.

HATERS: "Criticizing others is not always justified. I mean, sometimes we're just being selfish, mean and get kicks out of insulting people and making them feel less-than. Some attacks are unjustified, unfair, and intolerant."

- **My Thoughts**: It is indeed remarkable how these haters condemn the very behaviors they actively engage in themselves. Their actions seem to embody the motto of "Okay for me but not for thee." Their communication style appears to be a forked-tongue hypocritical approach that contradicts their own professed principles.

HATERS: "This online space attracts certain demographics, generally those with low self-esteem, who are uneducated, and the psychologically damaged. Both the viewers and bad actors don't understand how the world works or how to do their own research."

- **My Thoughts**: Using the generic statements of my haters, they seem to allege that their victims and viewers lack education, suffer from low self-esteem, and have psychological damage. These haters claim that neither their victims or other creators, including myself, possess an understanding of how the world works or have the ability to conduct independent research. Speaking for myself, I do not fall into any of those categories. While some may have psychological concerns stemming from past traumatic experiences, labeling everyone as "damaged" is unfairly generic, very judgmental, and undeniably harsh. I also believe this book's existence more than proves my capacity for independent research. Hence, can we then conclude that their statement is merely a reflection of their own characteristics and shortcomings? I mean, one could assume that haters of all types and ages must have low self-esteem, lack some education, and are likely psychologically damaged because happy, educated, professional, and healthy people don't treat others like they do.

HATERS: "This online space created a vacuum filled with unscrupulous, ignorants, druggies, criminals, and other gullible, stupid, immoral hacks, tragedy pimps, opportunists, and bad actors who strive to make money and grow their channel because their viewers are easy prey and they can't find a job anywhere else."

- **My Thoughts**: I want to clarify that I am not unscrupulous, ignorant, nor have I ever committed the crimes falsely claimed by these haters. Moreover, I also have never used drugs. While I cannot speak on behalf of their other victims, I do not fall into any of those categories. As evidenced later in this book, my earnings on the platform are very minimal, and I have enjoyed a very successful international career spanning over 35 years. By contrast, many of my haters have openly shared that they are unemployed and have even begged their viewers for financial assistance. I have not. So, I have to wonder if this is just more self-identifying projection?

HATERS: "We know a few who hold PhDs that are horribly poor critical thinkers and horrible moral reasoners and that hold rather loathsome moral standards."

- **My Thoughts**: Given the rest of the video, I am confident the haters were referring to me because, in earlier videos about me specifically, those exact words were used. I agree people can hold impressive degrees and otherwise lack skills. I don't believe I am one of them and this is why...

As for critical thinking: while I may encounter difficulties in certain areas such as mathematics, I do possess the ability to think logically and systematically when it comes to analyzing information and making informed decisions. I prioritize reliance on facts and evidence over being swayed by emotions or persuasive tactics, which is why this book includes extensive supporting material. I avoid binary thinking and actively seek diverse perspectives while considering the nuances surrounding a given topic. I am aware of my own biases and take pride in my problem-solving skills when navigating complex issues.

<u>As for moral standards</u>: I do not rely solely on emotions, personal biases, or cultural norms when making moral judgments. Instead, I consider the consequences of my actions on both myself and others. I hold values such as honesty, loyalty, integrity, fairness, and respect in high regard. When faced with ethical dilemmas, I have the capacity to independently assess the situation and carefully evaluate its ethical implications. I do not knowingly justify unethical behavior through flawed reasoning, generalizations, or rationalizations.

In both cases, it appears that my haters were projecting their own characteristics onto their victims, likely including their own subscribers, rather than describing me.

HATERS: "It is important to exercise epistemic humility and approach the claiming of knowledge and influencing others with caution. It is not our role to dictate what others should believe or adopt as their opinions. Calling out individuals by name can have significant consequences. Ultimately, what matters is whether we personally believe something to be true, and it is up to each individual to determine for themselves the usefulness or validity of information they hear and read online."

- **My Thoughts**: Indeed. These haters who insult my expertise and accomplishments also claim to possess extensive knowledge about my field. What's more, as you will soon see, they resort to verbal abuse toward those who express support for me or my work, simply because of differing beliefs and opinions. Regrettably, the current legal protections seem to primarily favor the platforms rather than the victims, leading to minimal consequences for the haters, monsters, and creeps. They are well aware of this and as a result, feel empowered to persist with their relentless attacks.

HATERS: "We can try to teach you the heuristics [short-cuts or rules of thumb to simplify complex tasks or decision-making processes] that come from thousands of years of formal and informal research and mathematical and scientific thinking and philosophy, logical syllogism, and more but they take a long time to learn and are not easy and that's why we are consumer advocates."

- **My Thoughts**: It appears that these haters were targeting their own audiences, possibly under the assumption that they are lacking in education. While heuristics can be useful in certain situations, they can also give rise to biases and errors in judgment when people overlook pertinent information, make inaccurate assumptions, or rely excessively on stereotypes and preconceived notions. It is important to recognize the limitations of heuristics and to strive for a more comprehensive understanding by actively seeking out additional information and challenging preconceived notions.

Preconceptions are often formed based on prior experiences, cultural or societal norms, and personal biases, leading to opinions that are formed before acquiring sufficient evidence, training, or firsthand knowledge or experience. This likely explains the refusal of the haters to accept my offer to analyze their own handwriting or that of *anyone they choose from anywhere in the world*, with complete anonymity for the writer.

It appears evident that these haters, whom I consider to be misguided and malicious, lack full awareness of their own preconceptions. Their hatred toward me stems from their disagreement regarding the validity or application of graphology or handwriting analysis, which is my specialized field. It is possible that their negative perception is influenced by their past involvement with an unprofessional analyst or hobbyist, or with divination practices, leading them to categorize anything they don't comprehend in a similar manner. Regardless, their preconceptions have led them to unfairly project their biases onto me instead of engaging in introspection and recognizing their own lack of self-awareness.

Now, using the haters' own words, specifically *"thousands of years of formal and informal research and mathematical and scientific thinking, philosophical and logical syllogisms, and more but they take a long time to learn and are not easy,"* I'm going to address this as it pertains to my career field.

- **My Thoughts**: Graphology, a practice with roots dating back to the 3rd Century B.C., has a rich historical background. In recent years, *formal* research on graphology has focused on conducting studies using rigorous scientific methods in order to evaluate its validity and reliability. While certain studies have revealed correlations between specific handwriting features and personality traits, there are still doubts among many mainstream psychologists who question its validity, citing a lack of empirical evidence. Nevertheless, it is noteworthy that the Library of Congress categorizes graphology under "Applied

Psychology" and acknowledges it as a "valid diagnostic tool."

- *Informal* research in graphology often consists of studies conducted by practitioners, which often rely on anecdotal evidence or self-reported data. These studies may not adhere to the rigorous scientific methods required to establish the scientific validity of graphology and therefore are not considered reliable sources of evidence. However, it is important not to underestimate the value of firsthand testimonials, as they can provide valuable insights and perspectives from individuals who have personally experienced the effects of professional graphology.

- *Mathematical and scientific thinking* are integral to evaluating the validity and reliability of graphology. It is through critical analysis and rigorous scientific examination that a clearer understanding of graphology's effectiveness can be achieved.

- *Philosophical* and *logical syllogisms* are employed to evaluate the logical connection between handwriting features and the revelation of personality traits. These syllogisms provide valuable tools for assessing the logical structure and foundation of the practice. By employing philosophical and logical analysis, one can examine the coherence and soundness of the arguments and reasoning used in graphology.

Graphology integrates philosophical and empirical approaches to identify and analyze different handwriting features, including size, shape, spacing, and pressure, with the aim of uncovering potential correlations with personality traits. Respected experts, such as myself, prioritize the use of rigorous scientific methods over relying solely on intuition or subjective interpretations. *More on this coming up.*

- As for *"taking a long time to learn…and it's not easy"*, it is the same with graphology or handwriting analysis. I make it look easy but it's taken me over three decades to get to my level of skill and accuracy.
- Finally, as for *"consumer advocates"* … throughout my entire career in graphology, including in my books, my main objective has been to assist and support others by giving them an additional tool to help keep them safe. In my perspective, I have consistently served as an advocate. In this particular book, I am an advocate for the victims by exposing the hypocrisy prevalent among the haters, monsters, and creeps that lurk in the underbelly of the internet. By doing so, I shed light on their actions and bring attention to the injustices they perpetrate.

The validity of graphology often sparks debates due to multiple schools of thought within the field and the negative influence of individuals who combine graphology with divination practices. These factors contribute to the ongoing discussion regarding its credibility. Regrettably, the actions of these individuals, whom I consider true charlatans, have had detrimental effects on professionals like myself. Hence, I have consistently advocated for government regulation in the field of graphology.

It is important to note that the haters who attack me and undermine the credibility of graphology, likely lack firsthand experience with *professional* graphology. Despite their claims of extensive research, mathematical and scientific thinking, and logical syllogisms in their respective fields, their biased behavior is evident. They lack objectivity and fairness, leading to unwarranted criticism. Regardless of the topic of disagreement, their actions undermine the reputations of all adults they target.

HATERS: "You don't want to be as bad as the bad actors just because you don't like them. We have a strict bar to measure bad actors' behavior that we consider harmful and dangerous."

- **My Thoughts**: Despite the claims made by these haters that I am "harmful and dangerous," it is crucial to emphasize that for over 35 years, I have collaborated closely with international law enforcement agencies without facing any legal repercussions such as court trials or imprisonment. On the contrary, my extensive experience and expertise have earned me a strong reputation as a highly respected trainer and consultant, with outstanding references to support these claims. Therefore, it becomes evident that the haters may actually be the ones displaying questionable behavior. It seems that they are unable to recognize the inconsistencies and flaws in their own actions, so apparently their 'strict bars' are invisible to them.

HATERS: "Mozelle says she only analyzes the person behind the pen, not the specific person as claimed, but that doesn't make sense."

- **My Thoughts**: When conducting handwriting analysis, it is important to acknowledge that without credible sources, such as the police, lawyers, or courts, to confirm the chain of custody, I cannot definitively determine the authorship of a sample.

This applies whether the sample comes from Joe Rogan, Rihanna, or the mailman, unless I have known original samples for comparison. That is why I approach each analysis by treating the handwriting sample as "anonymous." This approach allows me to focus on deciphering the personality traits expressed through the writing, rather than attributing it to a specific person. By doing so, my results remain unbiased, regardless of whether the samples were genuinely written by the individuals in question or someone else entirely. This approach also helps mitigate the risk of false accusations that the haters, monsters, and creeps would attempt to use against me.

HATERS: "We are not like a lot of people. We're here to call out harmful people like pedophiles, murderers, and those who commit serial defamation. We don't just pick random people to go after."

- **My Thoughts**: It is important to highlight that these haters should take a closer look at their own actions. A substantial portion of their extensive video collection, which spans well over 500 hours, is filled with defamatory content specifically targeting me, my colleagues, and other individuals who I personally have no knowledge of. These videos are fueled by hatred and negativity. While I cannot speak for others, I can confidently say that I do not fall into any of the categories. Their continuous focus on spreading lies and committing cyber-defamation raises serious questions about their true intentions and motivations.

HATERS: "We are social animals who are obsessed about what all other social animals are doing and it makes us feel better when the others behave badly because we experience joy in mocking another human being."

- **My Thoughts**: Indeed, it is true that some individuals may experience a temporary boost in their self-image when they engage in mocking or derogatory behavior towards others. This pattern is commonly observed among those who have low self-esteem or harbor feelings of insecurity. It is interesting to note that this behavior often appears to be a form of self-identifying projection, where individuals project their own insecurities onto others. However, I believe that the majority of society still genuinely exhibits compassion and derives joy from acts of kindness and positive interactions. While there may be a vocal minority that engages in negative behavior, I do not believe that it represents the overall sentiments of the broader population

HATERS: "Mozelle claimed to be a psychologist but I can't find any of her educational background online."

- **My Thoughts**: I would like to clarify that I have never asserted myself as a psychologist. I have made it explicitly clear in written, audio, and video content that my professional background lies in the field of Forensic Mental Health. I specifically worked in jails and prisons and then as a trauma therapist in the private sector before retiring as a Clinical Director. It is important to acknowledge that being a psychologist and a forensic mental health professional are two separate career paths, and any confusion regarding their differences does *not* rest on me. It also appears yet again, that these haters underestimate the value of independent research or they'd have known that.

In addition, for nearly two decades, I maintained complete transparency regarding my educational background and career on my website. I ensured that anyone seeking clarification or with a genuine curiosity about my qualifications could easily access this information. However, due to the relentless attacks from the haters that began in November 2022, my legal team advised me to remove the full transparency to prevent others from being targeted due to their association with me, similar to what I experienced due to my association with the detective. Despite this, I am still open to engaging with individuals who have a legitimate need-to-know and I am more than willing to provide the necessary evidence to substantiate my formal education.

HATERS: "This space [YouTube] is increasingly toxic and there appears to be no end to the lack of ethics, competence, and professional integrity. We would like to leave this space and never look back."

- **My Thoughts**: I share the same viewpoint as these haters, which is why, once this book is published, my channel will primarily serve as an archive, unless I decide to completely delete it all. However, it is disheartening to witness these haters perpetuate a toxic environment by displaying their own unethical behavior and lack of professional and personal integrity. Their actions involve engaging in spiteful and aggressive attacks against individuals who are accomplished and seeking to provide a fun, entertaining, and educational channel. It is important to note that no ethical guidelines ever endorse or consider it acceptable to engage in name-calling, cyber defamation, or any other form of toxic rhetoric. I strongly urge them to either leave forever or reorient the mission of their shows toward a focus on helping others rather than destroying lives. I believe that creating positive and supportive online environments can have a far greater impact.

HATERS: "If you are going to go after someone, be sure to appeal to facts and create a record of those harming others and doing damage to the world, because otherwise you are bullying and creating drama. Just because someone is dumb or misspoke, we're not going to make a hit piece of them for drama or attention."

- **My Thoughts**: I firmly believe that my intentions and actions are not causing any harm. Yet, I hold an equally strong belief that the intentions and actions of the haters are indeed harmful to many.

HATERS: "We have to wonder about those of us who stay in a tribe that is promoting less than admirable truth claims or contributing to bad acting or harmful behaviors. Nobody wants to hear that they are involved in a space with immoral scumbags."

- **My Thoughts**: I agree with their assessments. It is indeed reminiscent of the commonly used expression "the pot calling the kettle black." Their words and actions appear hypocritical to me as they criticize and condemn certain behaviors while being guilty of engaging in those very behaviors themselves. Sadly, it seems their viewers are still blind to the types of channels they follow.

HATERS: "We are consequentialists and utilitarians and we spend our lives considering the consequences of our behavior and words in public and what they can do to people and our society. The bad actors are not thinking and they are not careful about what they say and don't understand potential consequences of their words in public. They can get someone killed, pollute a jury pool, destroy an expert's or police officer's credibility, and more."

- **My Thoughts**: Are they trying to make me laugh? I'm beginning to question their views on reality. These haters have repeatedly attempted to destroy my credibility and that of their other adult victims. However, it seems that *they* do not live up to their self-proclaimed identities as consequentialists or utilitarians. If they truly embraced these ethical perspectives, their channels would not exist for the purpose of spreading hate towards others. Allow me to explain:

A consequentialist is someone who evaluates the moral value of an action based on its consequences or outcomes. According to this ethical perspective, the morality of an action is determined solely by the amount of good or bad it produces. Essentially, consequentialists believe that an action is morally right if it generates the most favorable outcome or consequences.

Utilitarianism is the most well-known form of consequentialism, asserting that the moral worth of an action is assessed by its ability to maximize overall happiness or pleasure while minimizing overall suffering or pain. In other words, utilitarians believe that an action is morally right if it leads to the greatest amount of happiness for the greatest number of individuals, while reducing the overall amount of suffering in the world.

It is possible that these haters subscribe to a consequentialist perspective that justifies causing harm to a few individuals for the greater benefit of the majority. This reasoning aligns with the principle known as the "greatest happiness principle." According to this principle, the overall well-being and happiness of the majority are considered more important than the harm inflicted on a minority. However, it is important to note that this viewpoint can be subject to ethical debate, as it raises questions about the value and rights of individuals who may be negatively affected by such actions.

HATERS: "Pay attention and really listen to the people when they talk. They will tell you exactly who they are based on their words, attitude, and how they treat others."

- **My Thoughts**: It has become clear to me that the true personalities of my haters have been revealed. Surprisingly, their viewers seem to either overlook the transparent display of their genuine hateful selves or derive pleasure from witnessing the misfortunes of others, which is that psychological phenomenon known as *schadenfreude*. This behavior can stem from feelings of envy or resentment towards those perceived as successful (Garcia et al., 2018). Publicly criticizing and humiliating others becomes a way to level the playing field, bringing the victims down to a relatable level (Thompson et al., 2017). Furthermore, their followers may seek social validation and a sense of belonging by aligning themselves with a group of creators who propagate hate toward unsuspecting individuals in an attempt to establish social dominance or to assert power over others.

HATERS: "You clearly don't have any respect for fair use policies or YouTube's terms of service since you continually violate them."

- **My Thoughts**: Although my official handwriting analysis channel, Forensology, was only five months old when their hatred toward me began, I want to emphasize that I have never received any violations for breaching any terms of service, and this fact remains true to this day. Furthermore, if they would take the time to thoroughly watch every video on my YouTube channel, they will not find a single instance of me calling out individuals or spreading hateful rhetoric. This serves as further evidence that I have never violated the platform's terms of service.

HATERS: "We accept gut instincts like a medical doctor who interviews his patient and then diagnoses the patient from the symptoms that comes from what the patient tells the doctor."

- **My Thoughts:** I feel it is important to address a specific point raised by these haters. They argue that my success and accuracy in handwriting analysis rely solely on the information provided by the individuals I analyze, which I have already addressed previously. They also claim that this reliance on personal input renders handwriting analysis a pseudoscience without a solid scientific foundation, which I have addressed within this book and in the "Resource" section. As mentioned before, it is ironic how the haters contradict themselves by falsely attributing the use of gut instinct to me, *something I have never claimed as the basis of my skill,* while now supporting the use of gut instincts by the medical doctor (something I also addressed earlier). If it weren't for the harm they cause to their victims, their contradictory language and skillful use of a forked tongue would be quite entertaining and impressive.

HATERS: "You need to think about consequences of your words and actions and be a more moral and good person to make the world a better place. Think about what comes out of your mouth, the way you treat people, and the potential harmful consequences of your words and actions. That's the central things for the basis of all moral philosophy."

- **My Thoughts**: It is amusing to entertain the idea that these haters may all have multiple personalities (adding a humorous twist to the situation). However, it is important to emphasize that in all the videos I have watched, specifically those that involve discussions about me, none of them have demonstrated any of the behaviors or actions they claim. In fact, it's been quite the opposite.

HATERS: "Mozelle, if you remove the strikes against us, we can schedule a private chat where we can remain anonymous to discuss our differences and the common values we share."

- **My Thoughts**: When the haters suggested that I remain anonymous, I found their suggestion illogical. They were already aware of my identity, whereas initially, I had no knowledge of theirs. Given my uncommon name and public visibility, it was evident that maintaining anonymity would be impossible for me. Furthermore, considering the intentional nature of the attacks directed at me, I strongly believed that any audio or video interaction would be recorded and manipulated to be used against me. Hence, I chose to engage with them in written form, as documented in this book. I am a strategic thinker, not an impulsive or naive one; I fully understood the potential risks.

While I am aware of the full names of all the haters discussed in this book, I choose not to expose them directly by name or disclose any other identifying information. Just as they could have criticized the topic of graphology without specifically targeting me, I can write this book without naming them. The primary objective of this book is to educate people about cyber-hatred and advocate for the victims of such attacks. I believe I have repeatedly demonstrated which of us is ethical.

HATERS: "We find people we resonate with and can find ourselves caught up in channels in which we are least objective because we are less capable of noticing bad behavior of the creator."

- **My Thoughts**: I agree with their statement because, as I previously explained, the supporters of these haters have not yet recognized the negative behaviors exhibited by the creators they follow.

HATERS: "You have said that your field is science-based and are promoting it as such even though many studies exist that debunk it and you disagree with those who do not consider your field a science."

- **My Thoughts**: It is important to acknowledge that everyone has the right to hold different opinions, whether it is myself or the haters. My opinion is grounded in my training and extensive career in professional graphology, while their opinions lack such foundations. However, it is crucial to understand that disagreement should never justify engaging in hateful or harmful behavior towards others. Similar to many other subjects in the world, such as the effects of drinking coffee, the benefits of taking vitamins, the accuracy of DNA testing, or the efficacy of radiation therapy for cancer, graphology is a topic that elicits different perspectives and findings. There are arguments both for and against its validity. This is why I consistently encourage individuals to conduct their own research and arrive at their own conclusions. Ultimately, the only opinion that truly matters is the one we personally assign to ourselves. The "Resource" section of this book will serve as a valuable tool to facilitate the research process and empower individuals to make informed judgments.

HATERS: "You and your legal team need to familiarize yourself with YouTube's fair use policy as well as U.S. government copyright law and its fair use clause."

- **My Thoughts**: My legal team and I possess extensive knowledge regarding these things and, as a result, have included relevant information in the "Resource" section of this book.

HATERS: "You have failed to prove your stance to us, to satisfy your burden of proof and therefore your copyright strike for when we used your content was completely retaliatory simply because you disliked the criticism."

- **My Thoughts**: I want to make it clear that I am not under any obligation to justify my career choices to anyone, particularly those who have targeted me with vicious attacks, refused to disclose their own educational and professional backgrounds, and use cartoon pictures on their profiles. Additionally, it is impossible for me to verify whether they are real individuals or simply mindless bots. As the copyright owner of my video content, I have the right to report unauthorized usage, which is why I took actions that resulted in copyright strikes on their channels. Their violations of the law were evident, and it would be prudent for them to familiarize themselves with the fair use policy before making baseless claims. I want to emphasize that their criticism of graphology does not affect me. In fact, this book and any potential interaction with the haters would not exist if they had not personally attacked me.

HATERS: "We are consultants and political scientists who worked with government agencies for decades." *One hater even added...* "My partner is a [impressive title] and my partner's parents are [impressive titles] so I'm not sure you understand who you are up against."

- **My Thoughts**: The essence of the matter is that I was peacefully conducting my activities on my channel when the haters and their like-minded followers unexpectedly launched a vicious attack against me. I had not encountered any of them on my channel for over a decade until my appearance on [detective]'s show. It seems that all of them are grappling with their own inner struggles while simultaneously trying to intimidate me with their claimed credentials, even though they hide behind cartoon avatars and usernames. I want to make it clear that I am not intimidated by any of them.

HATERS: "We have been scientists for 30 years and are part of a large community that are on our side. As consumer advocates, we tried to warn you about [detective] but apparently you didn't listen and have had to suffer the social consequences and fall-out due to associating with [detective]."

- **My Thoughts**: Narcissists often present themselves as consumer advocates, positioning themselves as heroic figures who seek validation and admiration. They portray themselves as experts, using their knowledge and expertise to establish a sense of superiority and intelligence.

This allows them to fulfill their need for recognition while exerting power over others. It is worth noting that their words have just verified my suspicion that I was targeted due to my association with the detective, as they employed a "guilt by association" tactic. Could it be that these haters are narcissists?

HATERS: "Your tactics are a way to defend yourself like the [detective] did. We think you'd want to put yourself above that. We have facts on our side in our criticism of both of you."

- **My Thoughts**: Although I cannot comment on the behavior of [detective], I am grateful that I consistently rise above the negative actions and words of the haters, monsters, and creeps who continue on with their false accusations and baseless claims.

HATERS: "We have no personal problems with you, our criticism of you is not personal, it is strictly academic disagreements."

- **My Thoughts**: Earlier in this book I provided a detailed explanation of the distinction between academic disagreements and personal attacks. However, it appears that my previous statements may not have been fully understood by the monsters and creeps who have attacked me. Therefore, allow me to clarify once again just for them: *I am open to differing opinions about my profession, and academic debates are a natural part of any field. However, when the criticism turns into hurtful language, false accusations, and attacks on my character, it becomes personal. This is my only concern.* While they may claim that their actions do not constitute a personal attack, I firmly believe that anyone with an impartial perspective would agree that their criticisms have crossed the line into bullying, harassment, and other forms of abuse and mistreatment. Therefore, it is no longer academic, professional, or constructive criticism but indeed, a direct personal attack.

Furthermore, these haters have made false accusations against me and others, including claims that we threatened to sue them, doxed them, wrote hit pieces on them, participated in smear campaigns, associated with other YouTube creators they dislike, and engaged in "dirty deleting." I want to reiterate that I have not engaged in any of these actions. Prior to their accusations, I was not familiar with the term "dirty deleting," and there was no hidden motive behind my actions.

I am mindful of my online presence, and while I rarely comment online, when I do, I make an effort to promptly remove any outdated content to avoid misleading anyone. This is why I refrain from publicly wishing people a happy birthday on platforms like Facebook, as such a comment would only remain relevant for one day. I will provide further clarification on this topic shortly.

By responding with factual information and explaining their misunderstanding or misinterpretation of my actions, my intention is to maintain my integrity and counteract baseless allegations.

HATERS: "Your business name of Forensology sounds like a cult like Scientology where you are combining a legitimate science word or partial word with the *ology* of mental health. That in and of itself is dishonest to your followers."

- **My Thoughts**: It seems that the haters are seeking reasons to criticize without fully understanding the context. While I am not obligated to explain my business decisions to them, if they had genuinely wanted to know the origin of the name, they could have simply asked. Despite the fact that they did not watch my video on my YouTube channel where I explained it in detail, I will provide a brief summary here. During my early teenage years, while contemplating my career path, I playfully mentioned the term "forensology" to my father. It was a term I innocently and impulsively created without any knowledge of the word "cult" or "Scientology." Essentially, I coined the term "forensology" in 1977, and I possess evidence to support that claim. The term stuck with me, and when I established my business after a brief period in the military, I decided to retain it. It is crucial to note that the name I chose for my business has no hidden agenda; it was a personal choice made during my youth. I hope this explanation dispels any misunderstandings about the origin and meaning of the name.

HATERS: "We want to publicly announce that we are being harassed and intimidated in real life by _____, _____, _____, _____, [detective], and Dr. Mozelle Martin with an organized smear campaign, cyberbullying, criminal threats, intimidation, doxing, swatting, defamation, and lies, all in an effort to silence us because we simply criticized them. This is despicable desperation."

- **My Thoughts**: Again, I cannot speak on behalf of others, but personally, I want to clarify that I have never engaged in any of the actions they mentioned. This fact has been repeatedly demonstrated on my channel, through my posts, and clearly stated in this book. However, it is worth noting that they have actually carried out most, if not all, of the behaviors they accused me and their other victims of. I believe that their actions bear a striking resemblance to despicable desperation, and I possess a comprehensive collection of evidence to support this belief. What is very intriguing is that whenever their victims begin to defend themselves, the haters immediately portray *themselves* as the victims and publicly seek sympathy. This tactic serves only to manipulate the situation so that we, the true victims, appear as the haters when, in reality, nothing could be further from the truth.

HATERS: "In your autobiography you discuss spirituality and therefore that is proof your work is not science but a woo-woo pseudoscience."

- **My Thoughts**: It seems they have not had the opportunity to read my book, *The Initiation*. I would like to clarify that while spirituality has played a significant role in my personal healing, ancient DNA research has also been instrumental. Both aspects were necessary for me to address the trauma I endured over many years, starting from infancy. Within my autobiography, I delve into the process by which a child's mind dissociates from traumatic events as a protective mechanism against immediate shock. However, it is important to note that the book primarily focuses on mental health and highlights how untreated trauma can result in ongoing challenges in adulthood. Above all else, it is a mental health book that presents a comprehensive understanding of healing, aiming to inspire other victims to seek assistance in resolving their own trauma. It appears that these haters believe one cannot have a spiritual personal life while working in a more scientific field. After hearing them repeatedly criticize spirituality and Christianity, I am not surprised by this. However, my personal and professional life is a perfect balance.

HATERS: "We are social scientists, economics experts, and financial business consultants and we educate people on things in society to be aware of, things that can be detrimental to others who listen to you."

- **My Thoughts**: Social scientists are professionals who utilize scientific methods and theories to conduct research on various aspects of human behavior and society. They explore social structures, relationships, cultures, and other factors to gain a deeper understanding of society as a whole. It is important to acknowledge that, regardless of someone's claimed or actual expertise, resorting to name-calling or using derogatory language toward others is unprofessional. Professionalism requires showing respect and civility, even when faced with differing opinions or perspectives. Engaging in personal attacks undermines one's credibility, damages professional relationships, and hinders effective communication and collaboration. No wonder most of these haters are jobless and struggle with finances, as they have often shared in their videos. I have consistently emphasized that I have never engaged in any behavior that could harm others, while it seems each of them has. Therefore, their criticisms continue to lack credibility with the turn of every page.

HATERS: "We will inform our followers that we have reached a resolution regarding our differences, and as a result, they will cease any further engagement with you, as will we."

- **My Thoughts**: From my perspective, this situation can be viewed as evidence of a violation of the terms of service pertaining to group-mobbing and harassment. I do acknowledge that the harassment from the monsters, creeps, and their followers has indeed ceased. As of the time of writing this, a period of nearly seven months has passed without any notable disturbances. However, it would not surprise me if they were to resume their vicious behavior towards me upon the release of this book. Despite taking precautions to protect their identities, they are aware of their own actions and may perceive this book as an attack, prompting them to defend themselves. If history repeats itself, they may attempt to portray themselves as victims and create a video claiming such, seeking public support to boost their fragile egos. If they choose to do so, it will be their own decision. Their actions alone will reveal their identities in the context of this book. In the event they respond with hateful aggression, I will not engage further, as I have already dedicated enough of my time and energy to compiling the evidence and creating this book. Advocating for other victims is worthwhile, but giving more attention to the haters is unproductive.

HATERS: "If you are one of our subscribers or viewers, you might need to remove yourself from a channel if you see behavior that is consistently harmful or a lynch mob where you all sit around and bitch about the other channel that you perceive as your enemy while making fun of the enemy tribe. That's not very helpful."

- **My Thoughts**: Once again, it appears that the haters and their supporters are not practicing what they proclaim. Right after making the above statement, they contradicted themselves by advocating for the *"use of ridicule and shunning as tools to minimize harmful behaviors."* I have addressed this previously. I am starting to get concerned for their mental health. From my perspective, something doesn't seem quite right.

The haters' confusion sure seems evident to me. They seem to rely solely on ad hominem attacks, strawman arguments, circular reasoning, false dilemmas, and other logical fallacies that serve their agenda or current video. They take issue with my expertise in multiple *related* fields while conveniently adjusting their own expertise in *unrelated* fields to fit the topics of their videos at any given time. After 14 years of college, a Ph.D., 25 years of work in forensic mental health, and 35 years in forensic handwriting analysis, I would hope to have acquired a considerable amount of knowledge and expertise. It is only natural to expect such depth of understanding after dedicating significant time and effort to education and professional experience. In researching my haters online, I came across some of their resumes. Let's just say that it would be wise for their followers to do the same.

Dear readers, by now it should be clear to you that the monsters and creeps communicate with hypocritical words, questionable intentions, and exhibit a lack of self-awareness and accountability for their own actions. It is truly unfortunate to witness how much of life they are missing out on due to their narrow-minded and judgmental mindsets. However, if it isn't already glaringly obvious, let me further expose their hypocrisy…

HATERS: "The people we target have nothing on us. They just don't like being criticized so they make up things about us including making veil threats."

- **My Thoughts**: I want to reiterate yet again that I have never criticized any creator on my channel, nor have I made any threats toward anyone. However, it seems that the haters have misunderstood my intentions when I mentioned involving my attorney. I did seek legal advice, and they themselves acknowledged this in some of their videos. I want to emphasize that I do not engage in threatening behavior. I only make statements that I can support with actions or other evidence.

HATERS: "Pseudoscience thrives in a world of credulous humans but science doesn't know everything and is tentative and provisional so it can get better and improve over time. Science could be right today and be overturned or proven wrong later. We can improve on science and update it as we learn more."

- **My Thoughts**: It is interesting to observe that the haters have spent a significant amount of time creating videos to criticize my work, dismissing graphology as pseudoscience based on their belief that only science can provide comprehensive and indisputable validation. However, they now contradict themselves by acknowledging the limitations of science, its potential for fallibility, its capacity for evolution and improvement, and even the possibility of its theories being overturned. Once again, their double standards and contradictory viewpoints become apparent, revealing their tendency to speak with forked tongues.

HATERS: "We should believe in our gut instincts and intuition. We evolved those senses to survive even though science has taught us that both of these things can deceive us and give us wrong information."

- **My Thoughts**: As mentioned earlier, the concept of gut instinct adds another layer of amusement to this situation. I have already addressed most of this but would like to address one more aspect of it. Now they advocate for the trust and reliance on gut instincts and intuition. It is worth noting that they themselves stated that science has taught us that instincts can deceive and provide incorrect information. From my experience in behavioral science, it has become evident that people can also deceive and provide erroneous information, just as these haters have repeatedly demonstrated in their content. Once again, their contradictory views expose their double standards. Perhaps they should seek a career in politics (injecting humor).

HATERS: "These harmful creators need to learn how to be careful and sensitive to humans. They really do need a basic skillset of compassion to have a channel."

- **My Thoughts**: It is ironic that as creators themselves, these haters showcase a notable lack of care or sensitivity towards the individuals they victimize. This lack of compassion becomes evident through their commitment of over 500 hours of video content solely dedicated to criticizing others, including me and [detective]. Such a significant investment of time and effort highlights their disregard for the impact their words and actions have on others.

HATERS: "We're here because of so many liars, frauds, snake-oil salesman, grifters, tragedy pimps, bad actors, and charlatans in this space. Those we criticize are bad actors who only post content to get likes, views, and money without true concern for anyone. They are unscrupulous and ignorant just to grow their channels and make money."

- **My Thoughts**: To clarify, I want to emphasize that my earnings from YouTube are extremely low, as will be demonstrated in this book. The reason for this is that my content is not meant to be sensational, provocative, or focused on creating drama. It is likely that the minimal earnings are a result of this approach. I am not motivated by the pursuit of likes, views, or financial gain. However, it is worth noting that these individuals who criticize me are once again accusing me and others of deliberately seeking drama to gain popularity, engagement, and financial benefits. While I cannot speak for others, it appears that their criticisms reflect their own behavior and reveal their true nature. Moreover, if YouTube is primarily promoting videos that are sensational or filled with drama, I no longer wish to be associated with their platform. I have no interest in supporting any person or company, either online or offline, that endorses and rewards hateful rhetoric and actions.

HATERS: "We are here to be a counterforce for these dangerous channel creators who operate on dishonest and deceptive tactics and we don't like people getting duped."

- **My Thoughts**: While I cannot speak on behalf of others who have been targeted by them, I want to strongly emphasize that their accusations are not applicable to me. In case I have not made it absolutely clear already, I do not engage in dangerous, dishonest, or deceptive practices. I do not partake in any form of deception or trickery. It is disheartening to see that the haters who criticize me are the ones who seem to engage in such behaviors.

HATERS: "As humanists, we believe in facts and higher standards of ethics and we believe in challenging people who don't. These bad actors manipulate and take advantage of people and they have thousands and even millions of subscribers and it's unfair to those of us with smaller channels who mean well."

- **My Thoughts**: I would like to address a few misconceptions in their comments. Firstly, it is important to note that being a humanist does not automatically grant anyone exclusive ownership of facts or higher ethical standards. These qualities should be upheld by individuals across various beliefs and ideologies. Assuming that anyone who disagrees with the haters automatically lacks these principles is unfair and divisive.

Additionally, suggesting that individuals with large subscriber bases manipulate and take advantage of people is a broad generalization that requires more specific evidence to substantiate. While there may be instances where individuals misuse their platform presence, it is crucial not to paint all content creators with the same brush. Many creators use their platforms responsibly and contribute positively to society, regardless of the size of their subscriber count. I believe I am one such creator. Success on social media platforms is not solely determined by the number of subscribers, but also by factors such as content quality, engagement, and consistency. It is important to recognize that those with smaller channels have an equal opportunity to create valuable content and attract an engaged community. Finally, it appears that these haters harbor bitterness, possibly stemming from their dissatisfaction with the number of subscribers they have. It is possible that their hateful content has played a role in their lack of success. In light of these points, I encourage them to reflect on the true intentions of their channels and evaluate whether their content aligns with the principles they claim to advocate for.

HATERS: "As socially conscious people, we take offense at so many frauds on YouTube from conspiracy theorists, psychics, dowsing rods, spirit box and tarot card readers, mediums, and others who claim to have skills but only humiliate themselves and manipulate gullible people and nobody seems to notice."

- **My Thoughts**: While I appreciate their perspective on addressing fraudulent content on YouTube, I would like to remind them of the definition of being socially conscious. This entails treating others with respect and empathy, even when there are disagreements - whether regarding career choices, hobbies, or beliefs. It is crucial to differentiate between expressing valid concerns and resorting to hateful behavior used to target innocent individuals.

While it is understandable to criticize misinformation and questionable practices, it is essential to do so in a manner that promotes understanding and constructive dialogue. Labeling people as *frauds, charlatans, grifters,* or *dangerous manipulators* without fully understanding the complexities of their work is often unfair and harmful. As individuals claiming to be socially conscious, their goal should be to create an environment where open discussions and critical thinking are encouraged, rather than being haters, monsters, and creeps.

The values of empathy, compassion, and engaging in respectful conversations are fundamental to a socially conscious approach. Once again, I encourage them to reflect upon their true intentions. It may be worthwhile for them to conduct a thorough inventory of their content to ensure that it upholds the values they claim to espouse.

HATERS: "Whenever we are desperate for answers, there is an opportunistic charlatan ready to help. We need to respect law enforcement and fuck everyone else."

- **My Thoughts**: I know my haters are not referring to me because I am neither opportunistic or a charlatan. I hold integrity in high regard and do not engage in taking advantage of others or pretending to be someone I'm not. However, I want to reiterate my belief that it is crucial to extend respect and fairness to anyone we disagree with, not just in the context of law enforcement. In any profession or field, there are individuals who uphold ethical standards and act with integrity, and those who manipulate, exploit, or cause harm to others. This can be observed even by simply watching YouTube, as creators vary greatly in their behavior and values.

HATERS: "Sometimes we may never know the truth and sometimes we should just be okay with not knowing."

- **My Thoughts**: I firmly believe in finding a balance between embracing uncertainty and seeking truth. However, it is equally important to approach discussions with humility, open-mindedness, and empathy. The pursuit of knowledge and understanding should enrich our lives and contribute to personal and collective growth. Nevertheless, I have concerns regarding the hateful nature of their content. In my opinion, their claims of superiority in intelligence, ethics, and truthfulness contradict my personal experiences with each of them. Engaging in cyberbullying and fostering a superiority complex hinder constructive dialogue and personal development. It is crucial, as their spiteful videos often emphasize, to acknowledge the impact our words can have on others. Therefore, once again, I strongly urge them to reflect on the consequences of their actions and consider the potential harm they have inflicted upon their intended victims through their written, audio, and video content across various platforms.

HATERS: "If you believe in body language or handwriting analysis, you are getting duped but you accept their authority because of impressive credentials even though they don't have the integrity to answer your questions. They just expect you to believe them and they are obviously driven by popularity and material acquisitions."

- **My Thoughts:** I strongly believe in the importance of evaluating the credentials of experts when it comes to questioning their ethics, principles, or methodologies. In line with this, I had maintained a publicly accessible 50-page reference list on my website for over 20 years, adding and updating as needed. However, due to harassment and false accusations, my legal team advised me to remove the references in order to protect the privacy of these individuals, many of whom were law enforcement professionals. Instead of making generalizations or assumptions about the motivations and intentions of any expert, I encourage individuals to reach out privately to ask relevant questions, just as they could have done with me. Approaching questions with an open mind and a genuine willingness to understand the perspective of their victims would have fostered a more balanced and well-informed discussion. By making sweeping statements about our motivations and attributing our actions solely to popularity or material acquisitions, the haters are behaving unethically and unfairly. I always welcome respectful questions and dialogue, regardless of agreement. However, I will not tolerate disrespect or vicious personal attacks.

HATERS: "Because we researched handwriting analysis online, we know you can't tell personality by handwriting and we believe in freedom of speech but she is tricking people into believing that she is helping law enforcement and that is what we don't agree with. The same detective with his skills is doing the same thing. I know that their other critics think they are very smart but most people can think for themselves and none of the critics should dictate what we watch or believe. They may be stomping on their viewer's constitutional rights. I don't want or need anyone telling me who or what to watch. If we don't like someone's content, we shouldn't watch it and should get a thicker skin because we can't go through life kicking people off of social media because we disagree with them. Other creators who jump on board with these other critics need to be careful too. People have a right to have a channel and just because we don't like it doesn't mean they can't have it."

- **My Thoughts**: I understand the concerns they may have regarding handwriting analysis and its ability to determine someone's personality, as there are varying opinions on this topic. This underscores the importance of learning from reputable professionals who uphold personal and professional ethics and possess quality training, references, and credentials. However, it seems that the haters who criticize me dismiss my field of work without firsthand experience. When it comes to freedom of speech, it is crucial to recognize that individuals have the right to express their opinions and beliefs, even if they differ from ours. It is important to refrain from labeling someone's work as deceptive solely because their career field does not align with our often-biased views. In order to foster constructive dialogue, it is essential to approach differing perspectives with open-mindedness and respect. Engaging in thoughtful discussions can lead to a deeper understanding of various subjects and facilitate the exploration of different viewpoints.

If you genuinely believe that someone is involved in deceptive practices or misleading others, it is important to gather evidence and present your concerns to the appropriate authorities or share the links pointing to the violating content with the platform itself. Spreading hateful content online based on misinterpretations, assumptions, and biases is not the solution.

Everyone has the right to choose what they watch or believe, and it is acceptable to opt out of consuming content that one dislikes. However, it is crucial to distinguish between legitimate concerns about content and personal biases that may infringe upon someone's right to express themselves. It is essential to maintain a balance that respects freedom of expression while addressing genuine concerns with the appropriate channels and authorities.

All individuals should be aware of the impact of their online actions. Rather than resorting to censorship, hatred, disinformation, misinformation, or engaging in social shunning or cyberbullying, it is important to prioritize meaningful discussions and create an environment conducive to learning. By considering the consequences of our actions and avoiding attempts to silence or attack others, we can foster constructive conversations that promote knowledge, empathy, and the sharing of accurate information. It is worth noting, however, that immediately after their statement was made, someone said, *"That's why we really need to force these people off of YouTube."*

HATERS: "After getting doxed, threatening us with violence for a whole month, lying about us, petitions and smear campaigns pitted against us, and then finding out that investigators are examining details of our lives all because we criticized their behavior. Well, we don't like it very much, but all is fair in love and war. This is just confirmation on the depths these bad actors will go to try to ruin our lives and they are trying to get people killed. I mean they are pussy, coward, low-life losers. They are like [politician]."

- **My Thoughts**: I am truly sorry to hear about the distressing experiences they have had, although I'm unsure who specifically they are referring to since I did not engage in any of those actions. However, in such situations, it is important for individuals to address the issues through appropriate channels and seek support from the relevant authorities. Also, I would like to highlight that engaging in hate-filled content targeting multiple adult professionals can have negative consequences, similar to the situation they are describing. It is crucial to recognize that such actions may easily attract online and offline adversaries. This underscores the importance of engaging in respectful and constructive dialogue to effectively resolve conflicts and misunderstandings. In my opinion, adopting a more professional approach to align with their self-proclaimed "impressive education and experience," rather than resorting to personal attacks or name-calling, would be the best way forward.

HATERS: "We don't have to be so damned hateful. We can remain calm and help others and know there are consequences whenever we spew hate. Don't believe anything said when others are being hateful and attacking."

- **My Thoughts**: I find it very intriguing and somewhat amusing that a significant portion of their content consistently involves name-calling, baseless accusations, and vicious attacks directed toward me and their other victims. It is clear that during these instances, none of them were calm. In many videos, their aggressive behaviors included shouting at their victims through their camera. Using their own words, it would be best for nobody to pay attention to their channels. Well, in that case, I must say I fully agree.

HATERS: "There is way too much hate in the world. We hate but we don't publicly go after people. We don't make up stuff. We should all just take a step back. All this YouTube hate gives the platform a bad name. But we are calling people out. We're not like the others. They behave like thugs and it's no different than criminal behavior. We don't do that."

- **My Thoughts**: Addressing inappropriate behavior and handling such situations in a constructive manner is undoubtedly crucial, rather than resorting to hateful tactics. I don't believe I have acted like a "thug" or similar. However, I do believe it is important to set a positive example by avoiding behavior that resembles criminal acts, including online hatred. I still can't help but ponder the possibility that they may all have multiple personalities (again adding a humorous twist to the situation) because their understanding of reality seems to sharply contrast with the experiences of myself and their other victims.

HATERS: "Then there is Mozelle, a fraudulent person, striking the other haters down for proving she is a charlatan. It's not a thing to tell personality from handwriting. She's been all over her haters trying to ruin them because they exposed her as a fake and it makes her crazy."

- **My Thoughts**: I was taken aback upon hearing this. It's clear that the haters lack personal experience with *professional* graphology and have not received any *formal* training in the field. They seem to disregard the fact that not everything found on the internet is accurate. Furthermore, they have shown no willingness to engage in a conversation or understand my career. Instead, they have blindly joined a bandwagon full of hate and made unfounded accusations. I have never targeted specific individuals who criticize me, nor have I made any attempts to harm or ruin anyone. Instead, I write books. I am also not a fraud or any of the other names they have called me. On the contrary, my qualifications and achievements speak volumes about me, just as their hateful and unprofessional content speaks volumes about them.

HATERS: "Has their organization [a non-profit I assist with from time to time] ever done anything to help solve a case? No. They only claim to have done so. No, you can't tell if someone has personality issues by their handwriting. You have to read what they write for God's sake. She made a video retracting her Chad Daybell video and that's just unbelievable."

- **My Thoughts**: I want to make it clear that the haters have been misinformed, as I have never removed or retracted any video regarding Chad Daybell. On the contrary, I have actively countered and disproven claims made by these haters, and this evidence can be found on my YouTube channel. I find it surprising that someone whom these particular haters consider a friend has misled them into believing this false information. It seems that their understanding of my profession is extremely limited or non-existent. Their second-hand biased opinions hold little to no value.

HATERS: "Her doctorate is an applied ethics, how ironic. For her to double down on what she said after [channel name] exposed her is just the icing on the cake. God! That makes me crazy. Supposedly she's threatening legal action against her haters who have proof. She's just a bad YouTuber."

- **My Thoughts**: I have already addressed this issue to some extent, but it is worth mentioning that it is quite amusing to see that some of the haters who joined in on the hate-filled bandwagon happen to work in the mental health field. One would expect that their chosen professions would prevent them from engaging in such behavior and would instill a sense of shame. As professionals, they should have exercised better judgment and reached out to me directly for a constructive conversation. I would have been more than willing to share my methodologies with them. Unfortunately, they chose to stoop to the same level as the other individuals who spread negativity. This is precisely why there are videos on my YouTube channel debunking their baseless claims. However, it is important to note that these debunking videos never spew hatred toward anyone or call anyone out. The individuals involved know who they are, and so do their viewers.

HATERS: "She's making wild claims and trying to exert herself into a world-renowned case. We are very good at standing up for the truth and we want our viewers to know about this woman. What so many people like her are doing is illegal and they scream out their first amendment rights. We don't get our kicks targeting others but they are dangerous and they are making money and it's wrong."

- **My Thoughts**: I want to clarify that I do not involve myself in specific cases or follow true crime. Due to my significant workload, I neither have the time nor the interest to do so. Additionally, I have never

195

discussed or mentioned my First Amendment rights because I do not feel the need to defend myself. I find peace in knowing that I treat people with respect instead of spreading hate, and I have always strived to maintain integrity throughout my career. While they each commend themselves for defending the truth, it appears that falsehoods are the only things being spread. Their accusations remain unfounded and lack credibility. It is amusing that they claim not to enjoy targeting others, when the majority of their content seems to do just that. It is hypocritical to label me and others as dangerous and unethical when it seems that each of them exhibits those qualities. I am not harmful to others, but it appears that they are.

HATERS: "Mozelle is linked to [detective] and [department] and claims to infer personality traits from handwriting. So, we went after her pseudoscience because we don't need another bad actor in the true crime YouTube space. It's worse than the polygraph and body language, which may have some scientific basis."

- **My Thoughts**: The haters consistently make uninformed and contradictory comments. In several videos, they dismiss the polygraph and body language as pseudoscience. However, now they suddenly claim that these methods have a scientific basis. Since they appear indecisive about their beliefs, let me provide a clear comparison:

Body language, the polygraph, and graphology are all tools used to gain insight into individuals' thoughts, emotions, and intentions. While they all aim to provide information about human behavior, each method employs different approaches and varies in scientific validity.

Body Language: nonverbal communication expressed through facial expressions, gestures, postures, and other physical cues. It is a natural means of conveying emotions and attitudes. Key points to consider include:

○ **Objective**: Body language interpretation relies on the observation and analysis of a person's nonverbal cues to discern their emotions, intentions, and overall demeanor.

○ **Scientific basis**: Body language is rooted in scientific research and psychological theories, such as the study of micro expressions and the universality of certain gestures across cultures.

○ **Reliability**: While body language can provide valuable insights, its interpretation is subjective and context-dependent. It requires careful observation and consideration of multiple factors, as individual variations and cultural influences can impact the meaning of nonverbal cues.

Polygraphs: commonly known as a lie detector test, is a method that measures physiological changes in an individual's body, such as heart rate, blood pressure, and breathing patterns. Its primary aim is to detect deception. Key points to consider include:

○ **Objective**: Polygraph tests attempt to determine the truthfulness of an individual's statements by assessing their physiological responses to specific questions or stimuli.

○ **Scientific basis:** While polygraphy has a long history, its scientific validity is widely debated. Many studies suggest that polygraph results are not foolproof and can be influenced by various factors, including the examinee's anxiety or countermeasures to manipulate the readings.

- **Reliability**: Polygraph results are often challenged due to their susceptibility to false positives and false negatives. The accuracy of the technique is contingent upon the skill of the examiner and the circumstances surrounding the test.

Graphology: also known as handwriting analysis, examines a person's handwriting to infer personality traits, emotional states, and other characteristics. It is based on the premise that handwriting reflects underlying psychological attributes. Key points to consider include:

- **Objective**: Graphology seeks to interpret handwriting strokes, spacing, slant, and other graphical elements to gain insights into an individual's personality, mood, and other psychological aspects.
- **Scientific basis**: As I mentioned before, just like any topic, there are studies in support of and against it. However, let me explain how it works. Neuroscientists have categorized neuromuscular tendencies and linked them to observable personality traits. These traits are represented by specific neurological brain patterns that generate unique muscular movements, consistent among individuals with the same personality trait. Handwriting involves neuromuscular movements. When we write, our brain sends signals to our muscles, coordinating their actions to produce the necessary movements for forming letters and words on paper. These movements are governed by the intricate interaction between the central nervous system and the muscles responsible for fine motor control in the hand, fingers, and arm.
- **Reliability**: The best way to answer this question is through independent research and first-hand experience with a professional in the field. It is important to seek guidance from someone who practices graphology as a profession, rather than

relying on individuals who use it in the realm of divination. Associating graphology with divination can be detrimental to the reputation of genuine professionals.

To summarize, body language, the polygraph, and graphology are separate methods employed to interpret human behavior, and each has its limitations. The effectiveness of these techniques depends on the expertise, training, and ethical standards of the practitioner using them. It is crucial to seek references and verify the credentials of individuals who claim to possess these skills to ensure reliable and trustworthy interpretations.

HATERS: "We've looked into all of her education but her handwriting analysis is pseudoscience mumbo-jumbo like tarot cards, psychics, or astrology. They use a lot of tactics to take advantage of people. Now we do know that Questioned Document Examination and Medical Graphology is a legitimate science and are evidence-based and part of the forensic skillset, but graphology is associated with palm reading and ancient woo-woo even though a lot of companies use it for hiring. People like her offer very damaging products and services."

- **My Thoughts**: It is indeed ironic to claim that Questioned Document Examination (QDE) is a legitimate science, while dismissing handwriting analysis. Both practices involve the examination and analysis of documents to extract pertinent information, and both rely on knowledge, expertise, and techniques acquired through training, while following established principles and methodologies. The objective of both QDE and handwriting analysis is to provide valuable insights and conclusions in legal contexts. Thus, if medical graphology is considered a scientific approach for assessing physical health, it only makes logical sense that professional graphology be considered a scientific approach for assessing mental health and personality characteristics.

HATERS: "Mozelle said her lawyer admitted it was pseudoscience and did a quick video telling her followers that. Then she retracted it saying it was just a trick to get evidence against us. Then she did a video claiming it is parascience."

- **My Thoughts**: For research purposes, I did create a video with the intention of observing the reactions of my haters. Contrary to what was mentioned, my attorney did *not* advise me to do so. It was a deliberate decision on my part. I wanted to test whether their targeting of me would cease if I appeared to "agree" with them. However, their targeting persisted. In the video, I mentioned that it was part of gathering evidence for a significant project, and indeed, it was. This book represents the culmination of that project, summarizing the evidence I have collected. It is important to note that I do not say or do anything without strategic thought.

HATERS: "She and the others we have criticized have called us haters and cyberbullies and we think they are working on a "criminaling" project together. They are willing to go to any depths to protect their livelihoods even in the face of criticism. They even threatened to sue us and of course YouTube does nothing to uphold their terms of service and anti-harassment policies."

- **My Thoughts**: I must clarify that the term "criminaling" is unfamiliar to me as well, as I strive to use professional language rather than colloquial expressions. While I do not feel the need to defend myself against criticism, I am genuinely curious to see how they will respond when confronted with their own actions as expressed in this book. Just like a mirror, the reflection of their own words and behavior may not be to their liking. As I have mentioned before, I anticipate the possibility of further content filled with hate and falsehoods being directed at me as a result of this book. However, I want to emphasize that I do not engage in baseless threats and carefully choose my words. I do agree that YouTube lacks effective enforcement of its own policies. It is important for platforms to take responsibility and ensure that their policies are enforced consistently and effectively.

HATERS: "This is a call out to YouTube to do something about the incessant bullying, defamation, intimidation, and dangerous behavior others are doing to us. We have it on record, we have made a police report about their [me and their other victims] actions against us in real life. They have come to our homes, swatted us, threatened us, framed us, entrapped us, and lied about us and our loved ones. This is getting out of control."

- **My Thoughts**: It is indeed quite amusing. The individuals who engage in hateful behavior, whom I refer to as haters, monsters, and creeps, have invested significant time and effort into targeting not only me but also other victims through various mediums like videos, audios, and written content. While I cannot speak for others, I can confidently state that I have never participated in any of the behaviors they consistently accuse me of. However, once again it becomes evident that when their victims stand up to defend themselves against these haters, the haters suddenly attempt to portray themselves as victims, seeking public attention in the process. This raises the question of whether this is part of a "drama for clicks" strategy that many channels incorporate into their otherwise unethical agendas.

HATERS: "We think we need to examine Mozelle's educational history because the fallacies in logic that graphology uses in its thought process as law of similarities is sympathetic magic."

- **My Thoughts**: Instead of making assumptions or launching personal attacks regarding my educational background, it would be more productive to engage in a constructive conversation about the topic under discussion, which is graphology. Furthermore, I want to clarify that I began learning graphology at the age of 11, long before attending college. The two are separate and unrelated, and my college education does not deem it a relevant factor. Additionally, it is important to note that graphology does not incorporate the "law of similarities" or "sympathetic magic" in its methodology. These concepts are not fundamental principles or techniques within the field of *professional* graphology.

HATERS: "Mozelle deleted many of my criticisms of her graphology. But I think [another handwriting creator] is more harmful than Mozelle because of providing outrageously harmful psychoanalysis to a large number of young people. Horribly unethical."

- **My Thoughts**: I do not have any information about your identity, and upon searching for your username on my channel, I did not find any results. Therefore, I have not deleted any of your comments unless they were offensive to my community or unrelated to the topic of the video. In cases where comments are deemed irrelevant, spam, or contain hateful content, I classify them accordingly. It is possible that you were blocked by default within YouTube's system, resulting in the removal of your comments. As the channel owner, my goal is to foster respectful discussions and discourage hate speech.

HATERS: "We have evidence on our side and you have fabricated an organized, illegal, and dishonest campaign to publicly defame us."

- **My Thoughts**: I am not familiar with the specific individuals they are referring to. As I mentioned before, if the comment was directed at me, there has been a lack of evidence provided to support their baseless claims and false accusations. However, it is worth noting that there is substantial evidence from their victims, including myself, who have experienced harm as a result of their actions.

HATERS: "We have only been on YouTube for a year."

- **My Thoughts**: This is another falsehood because if you visit their respective 'About' pages, you will see that their channels were actually created 7 to 10 years ago.

HATERS: "All we ever did was ask her to address our comments about her field not being based on science, like an adult acting in good faith because it is our opinion that graphology is a dangerous pseudoscience and that she is not even putting up disclaimers on her content."

- **My Thoughts**: In this book, my channels, and other public content, I have consistently demonstrated my stance and integrity. Throughout my encounters with haters, monsters, and creeps, it seems evident that none of my interactions have involved mature adults. Instead, it seems that those who criticize me are incapable of engaging in professional conversations. Instead, they resort to name-calling and false accusations, displaying behavior reminiscent of middle school settings.

HATERS: "We take offense at being called bullies. We are not bullies. We are criticizing her field of work. Maybe people don't like our style but we have a right to our opinion about it. She also calls herself a body language expert but she's an expert in everything. Ancient DNA research is also a pseudoscience."

- **My Thoughts**: I want to emphasize that I have received professional training in body language and have even taught it at the college level. It is important to highlight the conflicting statements made by the individuals who criticize me regarding the validity of ancient DNA. In one of their videos, they acknowledged it as a "legitimate science," but now they dismiss it as a "pseudoscience." This inconsistency raises concerns about their position on the subject. Furthermore, I have observed their tendency to undermine my verifiable expertise in various related fields, despite their own claims of being experts in disciplines such as science, math, advertising, marketing, business consulting, and other unrelated fields. It is intriguing to note that these assertions often come from the same individuals who portray themselves as financially struggling, lacking transportation, living without heat in the winter or air conditioning in the summer, and who even solicit donations from their viewers. If they genuinely possessed such extensive expertise, one would expect them to actively engage in public speaking or publish books on their respective subjects, rather than wasting their time promoting animosity and division while assuming the role of self-proclaimed social media watchdogs.

HATERS: "We use words backed up by evidence and if you disagree with me, we don't care. We can discuss it like adults but nobody needs to get nasty."

- **My Thoughts**: I can't help but reflect on their motives, whether they aim to derive amusement or evoke disgust from both myself and their other victims. Throughout this entire ordeal, I have yet to come across a mature adult who demonstrates professionalism. Instead, I have been overwhelmed by an excessive amount of unpleasantness, marked by insults, malicious name-calling, unfounded accusations, and various other forms of online hostility. These incidents are supported by the audio, visual, and written evidence that I have diligently collected. From my perspective, all I have encountered are individuals who exhibit childish, impulsive, and hateful behavior that is unbecoming of individuals who claim to be educated professionals.

HATERS: "People make living doing this sort of thing to others and there are all kinds of online review places that review products and services honesty and it's okay. So why can't we review people honestly on YouTube videos too?"

- **My Thoughts**: I completely agree that online reviews can have a profound influence and impact, provided they are characterized by a genuine intention to provide constructive feedback. Rational and principled adults tend to place more trust and importance on reviews that are respectful, honest, and focused on offering objective evaluations, rather than resorting to hateful rhetoric. It is crucial to maintain a civil and

205

respectful tone when expressing opinions and sharing experiences, as this enhances the credibility and trustworthiness of the reviewer. Unfortunately, I have not come across any reviews from the haters that demonstrate integrity in their assessments of me or their other victims.

HATERS: "Our role is to bring intelligent conversations to our viewers to help them be a better consumer and to disable the bad actors and frauds instead promoting those who really do care. There needs to be an ethical treatment of others with a concern of not victimizing someone."

- **My Thoughts**: Once again, I am compelled to ponder their interpretations of reality and even consider the possibility of multiple personalities within each of them (again adding a humorous twist to the situation). This assertion seems to contradict itself, as their words consistently diverge from their actions. Their communication, directed at both myself and their other victims, unmistakably lacks ethical considerations and continues to retraumatize all of us.

HATERS: "Our concern is unscrupulous bad actors with no skills or ethics especially if they are monetized and have a large YouTube audience. They are professionals who exploit their credentials in a disingenuous and dangerous manner outside of their area of expertise and exploit others for attention and money. Our society is stuck in an anti-intellectual mindset."

- **My Thoughts**: Again, I can only speak for myself. I am not considered a large channel and I will soon show you the pennies I make on YouTube each month. I also do not exploit my credentials. In fact, I rarely mention them. However, the haters often mention theirs. I never speak outside of my area of expertise but again, they sure do. I never exploit others for attention. Again, they do that.

HATERS: "People who don't like being called out try to intimidate and threaten us but none of that is going to work. We've done this for a very long time. We have nothing to hide and we are careful and thoughtful in what we claim to know and our liberal democracy is under threat. We need more kindness, respect, knowledge, and expertise."

- **My Thoughts**: I must admit, comprehending their perspective on reality is quite perplexing. It is important to reiterate that I have never personally singled them out, nor have I made any attempts to intimidate or threaten them or anyone else. However, I have gathered substantial evidence that clearly demonstrates their lack of caution, thoughtfulness, kindness, respect, and other similar qualities in their relentless targeting of both myself and others.

HATERS: "We don't want to criticize and offend people for their beliefs, we don't do that in private but we do it in public. We are sick of bad actors on YouTube who only strive for clicks and money. They crowd out the good actors. We are not asshole know-it-all people but we have alliances from [a lot of name-dropping here] who are all on our side."

- **My Thoughts**: The victims, including myself, have become tired of their disingenuous performances on YouTube, as well as their content that is saturated with drama and hate, seemingly aimed at garnering views and financial benefits. In my opinion, it appears that their continuous references to well-known individuals indicate a lack of confidence in their own skills or professionalism. This raises questions about why they consistently rely on the fame of others to enhance their own credibility in the eyes of their audience.

When individuals consistently engage in name-dropping, it can often be attributed to a desire for social status and validation (Smith, 2018; Jones, 2020; Brown, 2016). They may mention the names of well-known or important people to convey their own status or association with those individuals (Davis et al., 2014). This behavior stems from the belief that such associations will enhance their reputation, increase social standing, and gain greater acceptance and approval from others (Brown, 2016).

However, it is worth noting that I reached out to several of the famous people these haters frequently mentioned. Although it took repeated efforts, it was eventually found that these famous people had no knowledge of the haters. This casts significant doubt on the validity of their associations. Of course, this information is part of the evidence I have acquired. According to Johnson (2019), it is frequently the case that the individuals whose names are mentioned are not acquainted with the claimant.

Psychologically, individuals who engage in name-dropping may exhibit low self-esteem or feelings of inadequacy, using this behavior as a means of compensating for their perceived shortcomings by aligning themselves with more successful or prominent figures (Miller et al., 2017). Research published in *Self and Identity* has shown a negative correlation between name-dropping and self-esteem, verifying that frequent name-droppers tend to have lower levels of self-esteem and a greater need for validation from others (Thompson & White, 2015). Not surprisingly, name-dropping has also been associated with narcissism and a desire for social status and recognition (Garcia et al., 2018).

Additionally, individuals with high levels of social anxiety may be more inclined to resort to name-dropping in an effort to manage their anxiety and establish a sense of belonging and status in social situations (Lee & Davis, 2016). A study published in *Personality and Individual Differences* has established a connection between name-dropping and social anxiety (Clarkson & Stewart, 2017).

Examining the context of job interviews, a study featured in *Frontiers in Psychology* revealed that while some interviewees employed name-dropping as a means of gaining favor and increasing their chances of securing a job, others utilized it to establish credibility and expertise in their respective fields (Baker & Johnson, 2018).

Interestingly, research published in *Personality and Social Psychology* found that individuals who used name-dropping to assert their status and importance actually exhibited feelings of worthlessness (Lee et al., 2016). In this case, name-dropping served as a compensatory mechanism to address their own insecurities (Davis & Peterson, 2014). This suggests that name-dropping may serve as a strategy for certain individuals to boost their self-esteem and feel more valued in society (Smith, 2018).

HATERS: "Fuck ethics, fuck feelings, just piss people off, pit everyone against each other, and they will get a lot more views, clicks, likes, and money. They should be careful, thoughtful, open-minded, and it should make us second-guess the way we criticize law enforcement or other experts."

- **My Thoughts**: This statement suggests that there is a belief that some content creators prioritize attention and financial gain over ethical considerations and empathy. These haters intentionally provoke others, exacerbate divisions, and exploit the ensuing interactions. It is recommended that content creators adopt a more cautious, reflective, and open-minded approach to their work. However, given the contradictory statements of these haters, it raises questions about when they intend to do practice what they preach. With each turn of the page, their credibility continues to diminish.

HATERS: *No quotes here, just giving a synopsis of something I witnessed first-hand...*

One of my supporters, Stacey, bravely defended me on the channels of the haters. However, she faced severe attacks in the chat room, being called worthless in terms of critical thinking and accused of relying solely on logical fallacies and appeals to antiquity. They criticized her intelligence, suggesting she should learn how to think and refrain from posting what they deemed absurd comments. They discredited my career field, labeling it as made-up Jungianism, and asserted their superiority in education over myself and Stacey, who is a long-time medical professional. They accused both Stacey and me of using fallacies such as straw man, false equivalence, and red herrings, implying that we lacked the ability to read, comprehend, or construct a valid argument to defend our positions. However, since we believed we had done nothing wrong, we felt no need to defend our positions.

Furthermore, these haters claimed that I have lied to my audience about the scientific aspects of handwriting analysis and accused me of resorting to ad hominem fallacies, emotional outbursts, and sophistry. They accused me of violating YouTube's terms of service, defaming my critics, and making empty threats to silence criticism.

In a condescending manner, they told Stacey and me to continue engaging in what they deemed childish, irrational, and dishonest games, while they patiently waited for her to apologize before banning her. They implied that she should feel ashamed, and that their decision to harass me would not be influenced by any intimidation tactics.

Lastly, they asserted that when I analyze old letters of famous people and claim to maintain impartiality and objectivity, it is merely an example of hindsight bias and ex post facto reasoning. They made all of these claims before concluding that our level of dishonesty was impressively high.

- **My Thoughts**: I am not going to defend myself because my reputation speaks for itself. I have never experienced an emotional outburst in public, on or offline. The last outburst I can recall was in high school. Yet, I remember the outbursts of my haters toward me on their public videos very well. Regarding Stacey, I can't comment since I don't personally know her. Per my legal team, I am unable to share screenshots. Nevertheless, I can assure you that Stacey expressed her views in a very respectful and direct manner, yet faced unwarranted and unjustifiable attacks from the haters and their sycophants. As for analyzing famous people, yes, I do have some prior information if I know who they are. However, many of what comes out in their handwriting are things that were never made public to my knowledge. Again, I don't follow anyone or watch the news.

HATERS: "Our role is to get our viewers to become more discerning and to stop enabling these bad actors so they can suffer social consequences."

- **My Thoughts**: In case my haters missed this the first six or so times, I will say it again just for them...

I understand these haters believe their role is to encourage viewers to become more discerning and to discourage the enabling of what they perceive as bad actors, therefore leading to social consequences. It is essential to foster critical thinking and responsible online engagement in a constructive and respectful manner.

Thus, instead of advocating for social consequences, it is more effective to promote education, awareness, and positive dialogue. Empowering viewers to develop their own judgment and make informed decisions will help them navigate the online world responsibly. Fostering empathy and understanding can lead to productive conversations and a healthier online environment for everyone involved.

Unfortunately, the fear of similar attacks often discourages people from speaking out against such behavior, causing some individuals to refrain from using their real names online. As already stated, I consistently include disclaimers clarifying that my content should not be taken as absolute fact. These disclaimers have been present on my channel for over 10 years, but the haters fail to acknowledge or even read them. Those familiar with my work understand that there is no need for me to defend my career or justify myself to individuals like them, as their interest lies far from the truth.

Before concluding this chapter, after 7 months, I decided to check on the channels of my haters. One hater has completely stopped even though a few hateful videos of someone else are still public. Others have continued their usual activities. Recent research suggests that attacking someone's beliefs can have similar neurological effects on individuals as physical violence. Ironically, a couple haters mentioned this research. Hopefully, these haters can now understand the impact of their actions on me and their other victims. However, they also mentioned the use of mockery, shunning, humiliation, shaming, and insults, stating these tactics are not the most effective. These individuals then said research has shown that, to change people's minds, we need to appear non-judgmental and non-confrontational. Well, it would have been beneficial if they and the other haters had realized this years ago. At this point, the best we can hope for is no more victims.

As we reach the end of this chapter, allow me to summarize.

I believe you can see how evident it was that my haters specifically directed their efforts towards me and consistently exhibited contradictory behavior. While there is further evidence available, such as additional hours of video transcripts, delving into them would only present repetitive instances of the same underlying patterns. In order to avoid unnecessary repetition and respect both your time and mine, it is appropriate to conclude at this juncture.

If you are reading this book, I believe you are a rational, compassionate, empathetic, and intelligent individual. Thus, I have faith that you can form your own opinions about the characters presented in these pages. I trust that you now have a comprehensive understanding of the social media monsters and creeps with keyboards who have maliciously targeted and attacked me and others. Through this exploration, you have likely gained insight into their distinct personality styles and capabilities.

Looking ahead, let me provide you with a synopsis of one of the conversations I had with YouTube support, emphasizing the importance of having readily available links and evidence before reaching out to them.

It is advisable to request an email transcript of any conversation on any platform you contact. This proactive approach ensures that you have documented evidence of your interactions and allows you to refer back to them if necessary.

Keeping a record of your conversations enables clear and organized documentation of your communication with YouTube or any other platform's support team.

Book Art by Mozelle Martin
(www.VisualDiversity.art)

Thoughts & Insights:

Thoughts & Insights:

A Conversation with YouTube Support...

During a conversation with Kai from YouTube help that lasted 24 minutes and 33 seconds, I presented evidence of multiple instances where hateful videos about me were reported a total of 113 times. I provided specific video links and cited relevant phrases from YouTube's policy to demonstrate how these videos violated their terms. Despite Kai acknowledging that threatening content and sustained, malicious insults based on personal characteristics are not allowed on the platform, these videos remained accessible and are still available today.

Kai mentioned that YouTube's team diligently reviews reported videos and considers legal factors during the evaluation process. However, he also indicated that in some cases, a court order may be required, particularly for defamation complaints.

In addition to reporting these cybercrimes to the appropriate law enforcement agencies in the relevant jurisdictions, many victims took additional steps by contacting the Internet Service Providers (ISPs) of the individuals responsible for these acts. Once discovered the true identities of these individuals, we believed it was crucial to notify their ISPs and draw attention to their harmful activities. Unfortunately, we received no response from these entities, not even a generic reply. This further highlights the disheartening reality that the authorities responsible for addressing such matters often seem uninterested or unwilling to take action.

Alternatively, it is possible that this pervasive cyberhatred is now seen as the norm, leading some to believe that it is futile to fight against it.

"Behold, the talented flying monkey recruited by their hater creator to spread kindness and understanding through cyberbullying. Truly an admirable duo working for the greater good of humanity!"

(sarcasm fully intended)

Why Victims Don't Sue

When facing online harassment, it is important to remember that the actions of haters do not define one's worth or character. Their behavior often stems from their own insecurities and the need for validation. Recognizing this can empower victims to rise above the negativity and find strength within themselves.

Dealing with online harassment requires different strategies depending on the situation. Building resilience, seeking support from loved ones, documenting evidence, and involving legal authorities when necessary are important steps in combating this issue. Prioritizing personal well-being and mental health is crucial during these challenging times.

It is important to acknowledge that online harassment and "hater behavior" are not limited to the internet, as they reflect broader societal problems. By understanding the psychology behind aggressive behavior, we can gain insight into the possible motivations and underlying causes that drive individuals to engage in toxic online conduct (Miller et al., 2017).

Victims should remember that they are not alone, and the actions of haters do not define their worth. Fostering empathy, promoting digital literacy, and advocating for responsible online behavior are essential in creating a positive and inclusive online environment.

While considering legal action, I consulted with two attorneys through my Legal Shield service, which saved me over $1800. However, I discovered that many lawyers are hesitant to take on cyber-defamation cases for various reasons. One attorney suggested pursuing a "class action lawsuit" if I wanted to have a significant impact.

A class action lawsuit involves a large group of people collectively bringing a claim against a defendant, typically used when numerous individuals have been harmed in a similar way by the same defendant(s). In this type of lawsuit, one or more plaintiffs represent the entire group, or "class," and work with their attorneys to pursue legal action on behalf of the entire group.

However, after researching further, my legal team found that the haters involved had no significant assets or financial resources, making a class action lawsuit impractical and ineffective.

Using YouTube as an example, victimization occurs not only from other creators but also from YouTube itself when they allow "hater" videos to remain online. This cycle continues when YouTube disregards reports that clearly demonstrate a violation of their Terms of Service and when these videos are shared and reshared and then monetized by other creators.

While pursuing a class action lawsuit is a complex and challenging process, I did find an attorney willing to take on the case. However, other victims I reached out to expressed skepticism about its potential impact. As someone who has always advocated for justice, I understand the difficulties involved in seeking legal recourse in such cases. Instead, I chose to save my time, energy, and money and write this book.

Here are some examples of legal cases and social media:

✓ There have been previous class action lawsuits filed against **YouTube**, mainly pertaining to copyright infringement and data privacy issues. However, attempts to hold YouTube liable for cyberbullying incidents that took place on the platform have had limited success. YouTube's Terms of Service prohibit users from engaging in harassing or bullying conduct, and the company provides policies and tools to enable users to report and flag inappropriate content because Section 230 protects them. I have to wonder if just having these "anti-harassment" policies are a mere formality and that's enough to satisfy the law whether or not they ever act on it.

✓ **Facebook**: In 2018, Facebook was hit with a class action lawsuit alleging that the company failed to protect users from gender-based hate speech, harassment, and abuse on its platform. This case was settled in 2020 for $52 million. As part of the settlement, they changed its policies to provide better tools for users to report and respond to harassment and hate speech.
✓ **Twitter**: In 2016, Twitter was sued by the family of a woman who was targeted by anonymous online harassers and subsequently killed in a terrorist attack. The lawsuit claimed that Twitter had allowed terrorists to use the platform to recruit and radicalize individuals. This was dismissed by a federal judge in 2018 citing Section 230.
✓ **Instagram**: In 2019, Instagram was sued by a student who alleged that the company allowed anonymous accounts to send her sexually explicit and threatening messages, leading to emotional distress and PTSD. This case is ongoing.
✓ **Snapchat**: In 2016, Snapchat was sued by a teenager who claimed that she was bullied and harassed on the platform, and that the company failed to provide adequate safeguards to protect her from harassment. This was dismissed for reasons unknown in 2016.
✓ **TikTok**: In 2020, TikTok was sued by a minor who alleged that the company failed to protect her privacy

and personal information, leading to cyberbullying and harassment. This case is ongoing.

✓ **Reddit**: In 2020, Reddit was sued by a former employee who alleged that the company allowed moderators to engage in discriminatory and harassing behavior on the platform. This case is ongoing.

✓ **Tumblr**: In 2019, Tumblr was sued by a user who claimed that the company allowed child pornography to proliferate on the platform, leading to emotional distress and PTSD. This was settled in 2020 for an undisclosed amount. As part of the settlement, they agree to change its policies and implement better tools for identifying and removing illegal content.

✓ **Ask.fm**: In 2013, this social Q&A site was sued by the family of a teenage girl who committed suicide after being bullied on the platform. This was dismissed in 2014 by a federal judge citing Section 230.

As per the Communications Decency Act of 1996, particularly Section 230, social media platforms are usually immune from liability for user-generated content. Therefore, it can be incredibly difficult to hold them accountable for such content.

✓ There are three examples of the limitations of this immunity: intellectual property violations or violations of federal criminal law, actively contributing to the creation or development of the hateful content, or acting as a publisher instead of a neutral platform.

While reporting harassment or cyberbullying on platforms like YouTube may currently feel ineffective, it is still important to do so. Laws and regulations regarding online harassment and cyberbullying are continuously evolving, and it is crucial to maintain hope that future legal challenges will emerge to hold platforms accountable for the harm caused by user-generated content.

In the future, there may be consequences for individuals engaging in such behavior, including the retroactive removal of hateful content, penalties for host channels by the platform or law enforcement, and increased advocacy for future victims. These perpetrators could even face real-life repercussions such as job loss (Clarkson, 2017).

Through the process of writing this book and gaining insights into the true nature and possible mindsets of social media monsters and creeps with keyboards, I have found empowerment in bringing this chapter of my life to a close, and I hope you did too.

Furthermore, my hope is that by sharing my experiences, I can assist other victims in navigating similar challenges and encourage them to find their own path to healing.

Thoughts & Insights:

How to Survive Creeps with Keyboards

Digital Detox & Reputation Management

In the modern digital era, cyberhatred has emerged as a widespread problem that impacts professionals across different fields (Serani, 2018). Given this context, I have consistently made efforts to maintain a clean online presence.

As previously mentioned, I don't comment online much because the comments become quickly outdated. It can be frustrating to discover a valuable link while conducting research, only to encounter an error message when attempting to access it. Additionally, the uncertainty of life makes me reflect on how future generations, such as my grandchildren, will perceive my online comments if I died today. We aren't promised tomorrow, so I firmly believe that we should strive to set a positive example for them, long after our time on earth has ended.

These are just a couple examples that highlight the importance of considering the relevance and longevity of our comments before we ever post them. Stop and think.

Therefore, this section provides practical tips and strategies for adult professionals to protect themselves and manage their online reputation effectively. In doing so, we can mitigate the impact of cyberhatred.

Acknowledging Severity of Cyberhatred:

The first step in combating cyberhatred is to recognize and acknowledge its severity. It is important not to downplay or ignore the impact of online harassment.

Understand that being targeted by social media monsters and keyboard creeps does not diminish your worth as a person. Their behavior stems from their own insecurities and issues. It's not really about you.

Taking Preventative Measures:

- **Keep thorough records**: Document instances of cyberhatred with screenshots, notes, and witness lists. This evidence can be useful when reporting the behavior.
- **Decide on an appropriate response**: Consider your options and choose how to react. Engaging in name-calling may not be productive. Seek support, consult with an attorney, or utilize creative outlets.
- **Report the behavior**: Take action by reporting cyberhatred to the hosting platform, local law enforcement, and, if necessary, the FBI cybercrime division. Consider reporting incidents to internet service providers (ISPs).
- **Implement protective measures**: Use platform features to ban certain words or review comments before they are visible. Block individuals and take steps to prevent further contact.

Cleaning Up Your Digital Footprints:

- **Prioritize privacy**: Adjust privacy settings on social media platforms, limit interactions, and keep personal information private.
- **Delete unnecessary accounts**: Regularly review and delete accounts you rarely use to minimize your digital presence.
- **Manage online reputation**: Monitor your online presence through search engines and use reputation management tools to address negative content. Remove offensive or irrelevant material.
- **Strengthen security measures**: Regularly change passwords, use a mix of characters, and avoid reusing passwords.

Teaching the Next Generation:

Educating younger generations about responsible online behavior is crucial. Encourage them to think before posting, share positive content, engage in respectful debate, and be aware of their digital footprint. Teach them about privacy settings, protecting personal information, and the long-term effects of their online presence. Teach them to stop and think and help them fine-tune their emotional intelligence. By all means, warn them about cyber-sexting too by helping them build and maintain their self-respect and dignity.

By acknowledging the severity of cyberhatred, taking preventative measures, and managing your online presence, you can prioritize self-care and create a positive online environment for yourself and future generations (Smith, 2018).

Following is just one example of why we should all be careful online; it's a blog post I wrote in 2022.

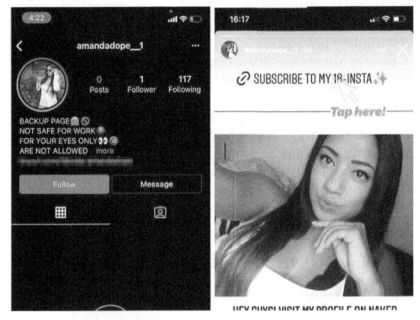

BLOG: Warning: IG Scam Alert

Recently, Malwarebytes posed a question regarding a hypothetical scenario where a friend sets up a NSFW (Not Safe for Work) account on Instagram and follows you. While social media platforms strive to capture attention and track user engagement for monetization purposes, it's important to be aware of the potential risks involved.

Certain websites, such as Dangerous Minds, BuzzFeed, and Bored Panda, publish NSFW content that covers a wide range of explicit materials. This can include vintage pin-ups, cross-dressers, erotic art, and adult-themed videos.

Malwarebytes shared the story of their former social media expert, Amanda (bitemycrust), who fell victim to a scam involving a fake NSFW Instagram account created using her images. Scammers attempted to lure her friends into visiting the fake account by following them from Amanda's authentic account.

Amanda's friends became suspicious when they noticed her face on the fake account but found the style of the posts unfamiliar. Phrases like "NOT SAFE FOR WORK" and "FOR YOUR EYES ONLY" were used, but no actual content was present.

Upon visiting the fake account, they discovered another stolen picture of Amanda with a caption urging them to access "exclusive content" on her "secret account" hosted on WIX.com, a platform commonly used for creating temporary websites. Stolen photos from Amanda's real Instagram account were surrounded by NSFW and pornographic stock art.

Given instances like these, some individuals, including Elon Musk, have expressed skepticism and advised people to delete their Facebook and Instagram accounts, noting that Instagram is owned by Facebook, along with WhatsApp.

To check if your pictures have been misused on a fake NSFW or any other account, services like TinEye (www.TinEye.com) and Google Images (images.google.com) can be utilized. These platforms can help identify instances of unauthorized usage, unless the content is deeply buried within the dark web.

Sketch by Mozelle Martin
(www.VisualDiversity.art)

Action Steps to Start Now!

✓ **Spread the news** about this book widely to show other adult victims of cyber-haters that they are not alone. Sharing this information is a loving and supportive gesture for other victims.

✓ Despite YouTube and other platforms seemingly not caring, **continue reporting** content that violates their policies. It only takes a few seconds. The more people who report the same content, the more likely it will be taken seriously.

✓ **Contact your local police** to obtain a report number.

✓ **Seek a free consultation** with a lawyer to explore potential rights you may not be aware of. Starting at less than $1 per day, I highly recommend using what I used... www.planoverview365.com/130735913

✓ **Share your story** publicly and frequently.

✓ **Seek assistance** from the resources mentioned in this book, both locally and online. I you can't find a local or online group for support, start one! Many churches and other non-profits allow you to use their space for such groups because it also offers "advertising" for them.

✓ Next, and perhaps most importantly, **evaluate your moral compass** and reevaluate the individuals you follow on YouTube or any other platform. Take the necessary time to review their videos, read their descriptions, listen to their words, and browse their timeline posts.

Using the list you made on page 4, ask yourself...

- Does what I'm listening to or reading make me feel *better* or *worse* about life or other people?
- Does the information that I am learning from that creator provide *valuable insight into my life* and / or give me *tools I can use* to help me make better choices?

- Do I feel *happy* or *relaxed* after spending time on that channel, or am I *emotionally exhausted* or *physically tense, angry, or otherwise feeling toxic or uncomfortable?*
- Does this creator *inspire* me to be a *better* person?
- Is this creator *building people up* or trying to *tear others* (including other creators) *down?*
- Read the comments of other viewers (their followers). Do they *support hatred by instigating* or *inciting* more hatred, or are they *defending* the victims?
- Am I associating with *ethical* creators, or am I *supporting cyberbullies and cyber-hatred?*
- Would my current and future loved ones be *proud* or *ashamed* of my online behavior?

Then, please unfollow those who perpetrate hate.

THINK BACK...

Most of us can recall a peer who was bullied during elementary, middle, or high school. Most of us know someone who experienced depression, struggled with drugs or alcohol, or attempted suicide as a result. Sadly, most of us did nothing to help. Now you can!

BE AN UPSTANDER, not a bystander.

- **Explore** the resources listed in the following section.
- **Share** your story publicly to raise awareness of this pervasive issue.
- **Keep advocating** and bringing attention to this growing problem.
- **Scrutinize** the creators and influencers you follow, support, or donate to.
- **Reflect** on your own online behavior:

232

- Are you an **upstander** who **helps** victims of social media monsters and creeps with keyboards?
- Or are you a **bystander** who **contributes** to the victim's suffering and becomes part of the problem?

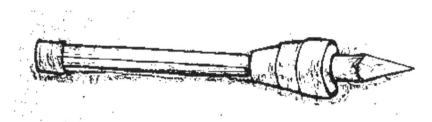

Pencil Sketch by Mozelle Martin
(www.VisualDiversity.art)

Thoughts & Insights:

Channeling YouTube

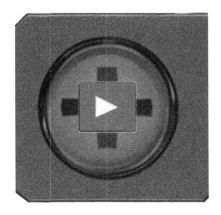

Considering a career as a YouTube creator?

Yes, it can be an exciting prospect, but it's essential to understand the advantages and disadvantages before making any decisions. Here are some key points to consider:

Advantages of being a YouTube creator:

1. **Exposure to a worldwide audience**: YouTube provides a platform to showcase your content to a vast and diverse audience from around the globe.

2. **Enhanced discoverability on Google**: Leveraging YouTube as a marketing tool can improve your visibility on Google search results, increasing your chances of being discovered by potential viewers.

3. **Access to qualified traffic**: YouTube attracts millions of users actively seeking specific content, offering you the opportunity to reach a targeted audience interested in your niche.

4. Potential to reach more people through YouTube Ads: Utilizing YouTube Ads allows you to extend your reach beyond organic traffic, potentially exposing your content to a broader audience.

5. Opportunities for repurposing content: YouTube content can be repurposed and shared across other platforms, maximizing your content's reach and potential impact.

Disadvantages of being a YouTube creator:

1. Hobbies become work: The demand for consistently creating new content can turn your once-beloved hobbies into a potential source of burnout or cause a loss of followers who may feel overwhelmed by the constant stream of content.

2. Developing a thick skin: The internet can be a harsh place, and handling criticism is essential. Thick skin is required to navigate negative comments and maintain your motivation.

3. Cancel culture: In today's social media landscape, there is a risk of being subject to the effects of cancel culture, where a single mistake or controversy can have severe consequences on your channel and reputation.

4. Privacy concerns: As a YouTube creator, your personal privacy may be compromised. Doxing, the act of revealing private information, is a potential risk that needs to be considered.

5. Effective time management: Being your own boss requires discipline. Without proper time management, the freedom of being a YouTube creator can result in unproductive days and a lack of income.

6. **Earning thresholds**: Accumulating a substantial number of hours watched or subscribers before earning even a few pennies can be a challenging and time-consuming process.

7. **Exposure to cyberhatred**: Unfortunately, the internet is not always a friendly place. YouTube creators are sometimes subjected to cyberbullying and hate, which can be emotionally draining.

When it comes to YouTube earnings, it's important to have realistic expectations. While some successful creators can generate substantial income, many struggle to earn significant amounts. Earnings can vary depending on factors such as audience engagement, ad revenue, and content category. It's essential to approach YouTube as a long-term commitment and be prepared to invest time and effort into building a sustainable channel.

In the end, it's crucial to weigh the advantages and disadvantages, consider your passion for creating content, and carefully evaluate the potential risks and rewards before pursuing a career as a YouTube creator.

As promised, here are screenshots of my earnings for two months…

Forensology with Mozelle Martin

Total Subscribers	Est. YouTube Partner Earning[Monthly]	Est. Sponsorship Price[Each Video]
11,000	$ 12	$ 5
	CPM $ 1.68-$ 5.2	CPM $ 25-$ 29

 **Studio**

 Forensology & The Write Story

10,981
Total subscribers

Channel analytics

Last 28 days

Views
4.4K ⬆

Watch time (hours)
484 ⬆

Subscribers
+5

Estimated revenue
$18.69

Now let's look at one from a popular channel that many of my subscribers also subscribe to...

Total Subscribers ⓘ	Est. YouTube Partner Earning[Monthly] ⓘ	Est. Sponsorship Price[Each Video] ⓘ
138,000	**$ 1,955** CPM $ 1.68-$ 5.2	**$ 1,401** CPM $ 25-$ 29

To reiterate, becoming a YouTube creator can present exciting opportunities, but it is important to consider the challenges involved. Factors such as personal resilience, time management skills, and dedication to consistently creating engaging content should be carefully weighed (Espey et al., 2013).

If you have a passion for sharing your voice and creative pursuits with the world, pursuing a career as a YouTube creator may be worth exploring (Forbes, 2022). However, it's crucial to recognize that success on YouTube is not guaranteed. It requires the right mindset, dedication, and a genuine connection with your audience (Clarkson, 2021).

Creators often experience burnout due to the pressure of consistently producing content, engaging with viewers, battling creative blocks, financial stress, and the need to stay relevant (Nelson, 2022). Moreover, when individuals are specifically targeted by cyberhaters, it significantly contributes to exhaustion and its negative effects.

From my personal experience, cyberhatred caused severe burnout and had a significant impact on my mental and physical health, leading to a month-long period of being bedridden. As someone with autism and multiple sclerosis, managing stress levels is crucial for my well-being. Therefore, I had to prioritize symptom management and take a step back. Unfortunately, my detractors falsely accused me of doing so out of intimidation. Many victims neglect self-care when faced with targeted attacks from malicious individuals; I wasn't going to be one of them.

Taking a temporary break from YouTube, even if it meant losing subscribers, allowed me to regain strength, write this book, and advocate for other adult professionals who have experienced or are experiencing similar targeting.

It is important to recognize the key symptoms of burnout, which include difficulty concentrating, anxiety, decreased productivity, eye strain or headaches, social isolation or disconnection, heightened irritability, and a diminished sense of personal fulfillment.

If you are a creator experiencing burnout, it is essential to prioritize self-care, establish healthy boundaries, and take a break if necessary (Radha, 2018). Your dedicated subscribers will support you when you return, just as mine did.

Viewers, if you notice your favorite creator struggling with these signs, offer them support and be an upstander by respectfully speaking out against all forms of online hatred (Patchin, 2020).

"When you're 40 years old, trying to cyberbully someone and you keep getting interrupted by your mom calling you for dinner."

(sarcasm fully intended)

Limits of Science Minds: Brain Capacity and Personal Growth

In conclusion, I wanted to write a brief section that examines the potential drawbacks of being excessively focused on science when it comes to the brain's capabilities and personal development. This is specifically for individuals who may automatically dismiss anything that is not scientifically proven with the claim that it doesn't exist, is not real, or is pseudoscience.

This specific information underscores the value of adopting a more comprehensive approach to knowledge and personal growth, one that goes beyond the boundaries of scientific understanding. By considering alternative perspectives, we can gain a deeper understanding of ourselves and the world around us, fostering a more holistic and well-rounded approach to knowledge and self-improvement (Jones et al, 2020).

The pursuit of scientific knowledge is a cornerstone of human progress, enabling us to understand the natural world and develop technological advancements. However, an excessive focus on science can potentially restrict our brain's capacity and hinder personal growth.

A significant limitation of excessive scientific focus is the potential for a narrow worldview. The brain has the capacity to explore various subjects beyond science, such as art, philosophy, literature, spirituality, and social sciences (Smith, 2018).

Neglecting these areas can restrict our ability to perceive the interconnectedness of different fields, limiting our holistic understanding of the world.

Lack of Creativity: While scientific pursuits rely on logic, methodology, and empirical evidence, an overemphasis on science may stifle creativity and imagination. Personal growth often thrives on exploration, experimentation, and embracing ambiguity, which are aspects not always prioritized in a purely scientific approach (Jones & Brown, 2020). Nurturing creativity is crucial for developing innovative solutions and embracing alternative perspectives.

Emotional Intelligence: Excessive scientific focus can lead to the neglect of emotional intelligence and interpersonal skills. Personal growth involves understanding and managing emotions, as well as empathizing with others (Goleman, 1995). These aspects of growth often fall outside the realm of science and require attention and cultivation to develop well-rounded individuals.

Ethical Considerations: Science provides us with powerful tools and knowledge, but it does not necessarily address questions of ethics and morality. Personal growth involves grappling with ethical dilemmas, developing a moral compass, and understanding the impact of our actions on others and the world (Singer, 2011). A holistic approach to personal growth integrates philosophical, ethical, and social perspectives alongside scientific knowledge.

Personal Fulfillment: While science contributes to personal fulfillment, it is not the sole source. Engaging with the arts, exploring spirituality, cultivating relationships, and pursuing personal passions are equally important for a well-rounded and fulfilling life (Csikszentmihalyi, 1990). Personal growth encompasses finding meaning, purpose, and fulfillment beyond the realm of scientific pursuits.

Science undoubtedly holds immense value, but to truly maximize personal growth and unlock the full potential of our minds, it is crucial to strike a balance between scientific pursuits and other realms of knowledge and experience. This means embracing interdisciplinary learning, nurturing creativity, developing emotional intelligence, considering ethical implications, and exploring a wide range of interests.

By adopting a holistic approach to life, we can achieve a deeper understanding of ourselves and the world, leading to a more enriching and satisfying existence.

The influence of science on society can occasionally have negative repercussions, and we can observe the lasting effects of specific advertisements from decades ago. Regrettably, individuals placed their trust in doctors (scientists), which ultimately proved detrimental.

243

Over time, it became evident and continues to be reinforced today that smoking is undeniably dangerous due to its significant association with various health risks and diseases, such as cancer, heart disease, and respiratory disorders.

As a personal testament to this, my parents, after being advised by a doctor to take up smoking, suffered greatly from smoke-related illnesses for many years before ultimately succumbing to them.

"Beware the cyber-hater lurking in the virtual shadows, masquerading as a monster with a keyboard!"

(sarcasm fully intended)

Resources

- **BullyingUK**: A charity that provides support, information, and advice to individuals affected by bullying.
- **Ditch the Label**: An international anti-bullying charity that provides support, advice, and resources to individuals affected by bullying, including cyberbullying.
- **i-SAFE Inc.**: A non-profit organization that provides resources and education to students, parents, and educators on online safety and cyberbullying prevention.
- **Legal Shield with Mozelle**: It is essential that you protect yourself 24 hours per day because you never know how far these *Social Media Monsters* and *Creeps with Keyboards* will go to harm you. Get access to a legal team like mine starting at $1 per day: www.planoverview365.com/130735913
- **No Hate Speech Movement**: An international youth-led movement that aims to combat hate speech online through education, awareness-raising, and advocacy.
- **Reputation management**: I have used the free version of www.BrandYourself.com since the 1990s.
- **Science or not?** If you are trying to decide whether or not graphology is science or not, I recommend the video on my channel or www.TheWriteScience.com
- **StopCyberbullying**: An online organization that offers resources and support to victims of cyberbullying, as well as education and advocacy on the issue.
- The **American Disabilities Act (ADA)** is a civil rights law that aims to prevent discrimination against individuals with disabilities in various areas of life, including employment, education, and access to public accommodations. While the ADA does not specifically address cyberbullying, it does offer some protections

for individuals with disabilities who may be victims of this form of abuse.

- **The Anti-Bullying Alliance**: A coalition of organizations and individuals that work together to prevent bullying in all forms.
- **The Center for Digital Resilience**: A non-profit organization that provides education and resources to individuals and communities to help them develop digital resilience and combat cyberbullying.
- **The Cyber Civil Rights Initiative**: A non-profit organization that provides resources and support to victims of non-consensual pornography and other forms of online harassment.
- **The Cyber Civil Rights Legal Project**: Provides legal support and advocacy to victims of non-consensual pornography and other forms of online harassment.
- **The Cyber Trauma Support Initiative**: Provides mental health resources and support to individuals who have experienced cyberbullying, online slander, and other forms of online harassment.
- **The CyberAngels**: One of the first online organizations to provide support and resources to victims of cyberbullying, cyberstalking, and online harassment.
- **The Cyberbullying Foundation**: A UK-based charity that provides resources and support to individuals affected by cyberbullying.
- **The Cyberbullying Research Center**: An organization that provides research and resources on cyberbullying and online harassment.
- **The Cybersmile Foundation**: An international non-profit organization that provides resources and support to victims of cyberbullying and online hate speech.
- **The Cybertip.ca**: Canada's national tip line for reporting child exploitation, including online exploitation and cyberbullying.

- **The Foundation for Individual Rights in Education**: A non-profit organization that defends the rights of students and faculty members to free speech and academic freedom, including in online spaces.
- **The National Association of Attorneys General**: Provides resources and support to state attorneys general in addressing cyberbullying and online harassment.
- **The National Bullying Helpline**: A helpline that offers support and advice to people who are experiencing bullying.
- **The National Bullying Prevention Center**: A non-profit organization that provides resources and support to individuals affected by bullying, including cyberbullying.
- **The Online Harms Foundation**: A UK-based organization that works to prevent online harms, including cyberbullying, online slander, and hate speech, through research, advocacy, and education.
- **The Social Media Advocacy Network**: A non-profit organization that works to promote positive social media use and combat cyberbullying and other forms of online harassment.
- **The Southern Poverty Law Center**: Provides resources and support to individuals and communities affected by hate speech and other forms of discrimination.
- **The Trevor Project**: A national organization that provides crisis intervention and suicide prevention services to LGBTQ+ youth.
- **WiredSafety**: A non-profit organization that offers help to people who have been victims of cyberbullying, online harassment, and online scams.
- **www.ic3.gov** is the website for the **Internet Crime Complaint Center** (IC3), which is a partnership between the **Federal Bureau of Investigation** (FBI)

and the **National White Collar Crime Center** (NW3C). The IC3 serves as a central point of contact for individuals to report suspected internet crime, including cyberbullying, online harassment, and other forms of online abuse. Individuals who believe they have been the victim of internet crime can file a complaint on the IC3 website, which will be reviewed by law enforcement and may be used to initiate investigations or take other legal action. In the case of cyberbullying or online harassment, individuals can file a complaint with the IC3 if they believe a crime has been committed, such as stalking, harassment, or threats of violence. The IC3 will review the complaint and determine if there is a basis for further investigation or legal action.

These and other organizations provide a range of resources and support to individuals affected by cyberbullying, online slander, and hate speech, including crisis intervention, legal assistance, education and awareness-raising campaigns, and advocacy efforts to address the root causes of these issues.

FAIR USE

Fair use policy and the U.S. copyright law include a fair use clause that allows for the use of copyrighted material under certain circumstances. Yet, there are limitations:

- Using YouTube as an example of a fair use policy, it states that the use of copyrighted material must be transformative by adding new value to the original work, and not merely copying it. The amount of the original work used must be reasonable and appropriate for the purpose of the new content and must not harm the market value of the original work.

- U.S. copyright law's fair use clause also allows for the use of copyrighted material for purposes such as criticism, comment, news reporting, teaching, scholarship, or research

It is essential to understand that fair use is a legal defense, which means that its applicability may need to be proven in a court of law if challenged. While fair use allows for certain uses of copyrighted material without permission from the copyright holder, it is crucial to respect intellectual property rights and take appropriate measures to avoid potential legal complications.

To gain a better understanding of copyright law, including fair use, individuals can visit the website www.copyright.gov. This website provides comprehensive information on various aspects of copyright law, such as copyright registration, infringement, and fair use. It serves as a valuable resource for creators and copyright owners, offering guidance and resources to help navigate copyright-related issues.

Furthermore, the website also provides insights into international copyright law, ensuring individuals have access to relevant information when dealing with copyright matters that extend beyond national borders.

When utilizing copyrighted material, it is advisable to exercise caution, conduct research, and seek legal advice if necessary. Understanding the principles of fair use and adhering to copyright regulations can help creators and users of copyrighted content avoid potential legal disputes and uphold intellectual property rights.

Thoughts & Insights:

In conclusion, my autobiography recounts my personal journey of enduring relentless bullying, which prepared me to confront the challenges posed by Social Media Monsters and Creeps with Keyboards. Instead of seeking revenge, I emerged as an advocate for positive change. Through my story, I aim to inspire others to find their voice and stand up against online hatred. Together, we can create a safer and more compassionate digital world.

By sharing these two books, we can work together to support one another and navigate the messiness of life.

Thoughts & Insights:

References

Bell, E., Kowalski, C. M., Vernon, P. A., & Schermer, J. A. (2021). Political Hearts of Darkness: The Dark Triad as Predictors of Political Orientations and Interest in Politics. Behavioral Sciences, 11(12), 169. doi:10.3390/bs11120169

Brown, A. (2016). The psychology behind name-dropping. Psychology Today. Retrieved from www.psychologytoday.com

Brown, C. M., & Williams, S. L. (2019). Gender and Online Aggression: Investigating the Role of Social Media Addiction and Antisocial Traits. Journal of Interpersonal Violence, 36(1-2), NP60-NP79.

Brown, K. (2018). Cyber-Hatred and Cyber-Sadism: The Dark Side of Social Media. In C.

Baruh, Z. O. Cemalcılar, & M. Keating (Eds.), Transforming Politics and Policy in the Digital Age (pp. 221-238). Palgrave Macmillan.

Brubaker, P. H., & Church, S. H. (2020). Schadenfreude, Trolling, and Online Communication: Enriching Versus Hindering Experiences. Journal of Broadcasting & Electronic Media, 64(3), 520-537.

Brubaker, P. J., Montez, D., & Church, S. H. (2021). The Power of Schadenfreude: Predicting Behaviors and Perceptions of Trolling Among Reddit Users. Social Media + Society, 7(2). doi:gov/10.117/20563512101382

Canaday, S. (2013). When Self-Promotion Crosses the Line. Psychology Today. Retrieved from www.psychologytoday.com

Cases, M., Frazier, S., & Thompson, J. (2011). Supportive YouTube Community: A content analysis. Social Media, 90-92. doi:10.1016/j.bodyim.2010.10.003

Cikanavicius, D. (2019, July 1). How Narcissists Pretend to Impress, Manipulate, and Use You. PsychCentral. Retrieved from https://psychcentral.com/

Clarkson, C. (2021). Cyber-Hatred in the Digital Age: Understanding and Combating Cyberbullying and Online Hate. Cambridge University Press.

Clarkson, J. J., & Stewart, A. J. (2017). Name-dropping in job interviews: An examination of contextual influences. Personality and Individual Differences, 116, 95-99.

Controversial Reality Blog with Mozelle Martin. Retrieved from https://t.ly/cmwM

Craker, N., & March, E. (2016). The dark side of Facebook: The Dark Tetrad, negative social potency, and trolling behaviors. Personality and Individual Differences, 102, 79-84. doi: 10.1016/j.paid.2016.06.043

Csikszentmihalyi, M. (1990). Flow: Psychology of optimal experience. Harper & Row.

Cyberstalking: An Examination of Gender Differences. In P. K. Smith & S. K. Son (Eds.), The Wiley Handbook of Violence and Aggression (pp. 1-13). Wiley-Blackwell.

Davis, C. (2022, April 1). How to deal with defamatory content on social media. Internet Law Centre. Retrieved May 1, 2023.

Davis, D., & Peterson, N. A. (2014). Using name-dropping as a compensatory mechanism to assert status and importance. Journal of Personality and Social Psychology, 106(2), 213-229.

Davis, S., & Jones, D. N. (2016). Cyber-Hatred: Exploring the Dark Side of the Internet. In R. M. Kowalski (Ed.), Cyberbullying in the Global Playground: Research from International Perspectives (pp. 101-121). Wiley-Blackwell.

Ellwood, B. (2021, March). Dark personality traits linked to compulsive and aggressive online behaviors. Psypost. Retrieved from www.psypost.org

Espey, K., Duffy, J., & Mc Guckin, C. (2013). A mixed methods approach to understanding cyberbullying: A role for both quantitative and qualitative research. Trinity Education Papers, 2, 112-126.

Forbes Coaches Council. (2022, February 11). 14 Mistakes to Avoid When Self-Promoting. Forbes. Retrieved from www.forbes.com

Forensology. (2022, December 15). Field Trip: Chad Daybell & Lori Vallow Handwriting Analysis (Debunking HTC) [Video]. YouTube. Retrieved from https://youtu.be/F6Wofys7EU

Forensology. (2022, December 8). December is Creative Catch-Up Month (Since 2015) [Video]. YouTube. Retrieved from https://youtu.be/AUBgVDZwh0A

Forensology. (2022, December 8). Handwriting Analysis Field Trip (Debunking the Haters again) [Video]. YouTube. Retrieved from https://youtu.be/5ryWmoTL60w

García, D., Rosenberg, P., Erlandsson, A., & Siddiqui, N. (2021). Spitefulness: An Overlooked Personality Trait with

Significant Behavioral and Health Outcomes. Frontiers in Psychology, 12, 707773.

Garcia, S. M., Weaver, K., Moskowitz, G. B., & Darley, J. M. (2018). Privilege from privilege: Contexts in which social status enhances the effects of power on prejudice. Journal of Personality and Social Psychology, 114(5), 643-670.

Gnambs T., Appel M. Narcissism and social networking behavior: A meta-analysis. Journal of Personality. 2018;86:200–212. doi.org/10.1111/jopy.12305.

Goleman, D. (1995). Emotional intelligence: Why it can matter more than IQ. Bantam.

Goodboy, A. K. (2015). The personality profile of a cyberbully: Examining the Dark Triad. Computers in Human Behavior, 49, 1-4.

Grizzly True Crime. (2022, July 4). Jealous YouTuber Almost KILLS Another YouTuber! [Video]. YouTube. Retrieved from www.youtube.com/watch?v=dlqzqFN6VsU

Hall, S. L. (2022, March 21). Trolls, Haters, and Abusers: What Creators Can Do About Online Bullying. The Tilt. Retrieved December 1, 2022, from www.thetilt.com

Hussain, Z., & Starcevic, V. (2020). Problematic social networking site use: A brief review of recent research methods and the way forward. Current Opinion in Psychology, 36, 89–95. doi.org/10.1016/j.coyc.2020.05.007.

Johnson, K. (2020). Cyber-Hatred and Cyberbullying: The Dark Side of the Digital Age. Routledge.

Johnson, R. (2019). No, you don't know all those famous people you namedrop. Wired. Retrieved from www.wired.com

Jones, A. (2022, June 15). The Laws for Cyberbullying, Harassment, and Online Abuse. Cybersmile. Retrieved May 1, 2023, from www.cybersmile.org/

Jones, D. N. (2015). Sadism and the Dark Triad. Personality and Individual Differences, 86, 360-364.

Jones, L. (2020). The name-dropping delusion: Why we think we're closer than we really are to famous people. HuffPost. Retrieved from www.huffpost.com

Jones, S. R., & Brown, L. (2020). The science of creativity: From potential to realization. Oxford University Press.

Joshi, K., & Chauhan, P. (2020). A Survey on Personality Trait Recognition from Handwriting: Approach and Applications. In 2020 3rd International Conference on Intelligent Sustainable Systems (ICISS) (pp. 321-327).

Karatsoli, M., & Nathanail, E. (2020). Examining gender differences of social media use for activity planning and travel choices. European Transport Research Review, 12(1), 44. doi.org/10.1186/s12544-020-00436-4

Kardefelt-Winther, D. (2017). Conceptualizing Internet use disorders: Addiction or coping process? Psychiatry and Clinical Neurosciences, 71(7), 459–466. doi.org/10.1111/pcn.12413

Kircaburun, K., Alhabash, S., Tosuntaş, Ş. B., & Griffiths, M. D. (2022). The Dark Side of the Internet: Exploring the Relationship Between the Dark Tetrad, Online Anonymity, and Cyber-Hatred. International Journal of Mental Health and Addiction, 1-16.

Lee, S. Y., & Davis, M. H. (2016). Effects of social anxiety and name-dropping on self-presentation in job interviews. Communication Research Reports, 33(1), 50-57.

Lee, Y., Chang, C. T., Lin, Y., & Cheng, Z. H. (2020). The Dark Side of Smartphone Usage: Psychological Traits, Compulsive Behavior, and Technostress. Computers in Human Behavior, 102, 65-77.

Lewis, J. G. (2014, February 25). Internet Trolls are Also Real-Life Trolls. The Guardian. Retrieved December 1, 2022, from www.theguardian.com

Martin, K., March, E., & Moore, T. (2021). The Dark Side of the Internet: Examining the Psychological Correlates of Online Misbehavior. In J. Hartlep, J. Chester, & A. Yeo (Eds.), The Dark Side of Technology in Higher Education (pp. 127-148). IGI Global.

McCullough, M. E., Emmons, R. A., Kilpatrick, S. D., & Mooney, C. N. (2003). Narcissists as "Victims": The Role of Narcissism in the Perception of Transgressions. Personality and Social Psychology Bulletin, 29(7), 885–893. doi.org/10.1177/0146167203029007007

Miller, R. S., Chance, S. E., Norton, M. C., & Fincham, F. D. (2017). Narcissism and celebrity. In C. A. M. Rojek (Ed.), Fame attack: The inflation of celebrity and its consequences (pp. 91-111). Bloomsbury Academic.

Moor, L., & Anderson, J. R. (2019). A systematic literature review of the relationship between dark personality traits and antisocial online behaviors. Personality Differences, 144, 40–55. doi.org/10.1016/j.paid.2019.02.027.

Necula, C. (2020). Journal of Experiential Psychotherapy, Vol. 23, No. 3 (91), September 2020.

Nelson, J. (2022, June 15). Cyberbullying & Abuse on Social Media. Cybersmile. Retrieved May 1, 2023, from www.cybersmile.org

Nguyen, N. N., Takahashi, Y., & Nham, T. P. (2022). Relationship between emotional intelligence and narcissism: a meta-analysis. Management Research Review, 45(10), 1338-1353. doi.org/10.1108/MRR-07-2021-0515

Nocera, T., & Dahlen, E. (2020, August 01). Dark Triad Personality Traits in Cyber Aggression Among College Students. Violence and Victims, 35, 524-538. doi.org/10.1891/VV-D-18-00058

O'Driscoll, A. (2023, March 21). Online hate crime statistics and facts of 2020 – 2023. Comparitech. Retrieved April 30, 2023, from www.comparitech.com

Owaida, A. (2020, June 15). Cyberbullying: Adults Can Be Victims Too. We Live Security. Retrieved May 1, 2023, from www.welivesecurity.com

Patchin, J. (2020, December 20). Advice for Adult Victims of Cyberbullying. Cyberbullying. Retrieved May 1, 2023, from https://cyberbullying.org

Patchin, J. (2020, December 20). Preventing Cyberbullying. Cyberbullying. Retrieved May 1, 2023, from https://cyberbullying.org

Patchin, J. (2020, December 20). Responding to Cyberbullying: Top Ten Tips for Adults Who Are Being

Harassed Online. Cyberbullying. Retrieved May 1, 2023, from https://cyberbullying.org

Petit, J., & Carcioppolo, N. (2020). Associations between the Dark Triad and online communication behavior: A brief report of preliminary findings. Communication Research Reports, 37(5), 286–297.

Radha, D. (2018, June 1). Two Takes Depression: Bullycide. Psychology Today. Retrieved May 1, 2023, from www.psychologytoday.com

Reed, P. (2019, September 24). Narcissism and Social Media: Should We Be Afraid? Psychology Today. Retrieved from www.psychologytoday.com

Serani, D. (2018, June 2). Bullycide. Psychology Today. Retrieved December 3, 2022.

Singer, P. (2011). Practical ethics. Cambridge University Press.

Smith, J. (2018). The role of interdisciplinary studies in broadening undergraduate perspectives. Journal of Higher Education, 89(1), 1-25.

Smith, J. (2018). Why do people drop names? Psychology Today. Retrieved from www.psychologytoday.com

Smith, R. H. (2010). Envy and Schadenfreude. Current Directions in Psychological Science, 19(6), 353–358.

Szabó, E., & Jones, D. N. (2019). Gender differences moderate Machiavellianism and impulsivity: Implications for Dark Triad research. Personality and Individual Differences, 141, 160–165.

Taves, M. (2020, March 19). You Can't Win an Argument with an Internet Troll, So What Can You Do? Webroot. Retrieved May 1, 2023, from www.webroot.com

Thompson, A., Voyer, D., & Saguy, T. (2017). Sadistic Tendencies: Moral Schadenfreude and the Dark Triad Traits. Personality and Individual Differences, 107, 47–52.

Twenge, J. M. (2014). Generation Me: Why Today's Young Americans Are More Confident, Assertive, Entitled--and More Miserable Than Ever Before. Paperback.

Twenge, J. M., & Campbell, W. K. (2010). The Narcissism Epidemic: Living in the Age of Entitlement. Paperback.

Wang, M.-J., Yogeeswaran, K., Andrews, N. P., Hawi, D. R., & Sibley, C. G. (2019). How Common Is Cyberbullying Among Adults? Exploring Gender, Ethnic, and Age Differences in the Prevalence of Cyberbullying. Cyberpsychology, Behavior, and Social Networking, 22(11), 686–691. doi.org/10.1089/cyber.2019.0146

Winter, S. (2015). They Came, They Liked, They Commented: Social Influence on Facebook News Channels. Cyberpsychology, Behavior, and Social Networking, 18(8), 431–436. doi.org/10.1089/cyber.2015.0005

Zajenkowski, M., Maciantowicz, O., Szymaniak, K., & Urban, P. (2018). Vulnerable and Grandiose Narcissism are Differentially Associated with the Dark Triad Traits of Psychopathy and Machiavellianism. Journal of Individual Differences, 39(2), 114–121.

Disclaimer: Due to challenges associated with my autism, I find it difficult to visually process the chaotic appearance of longtail URLs. As a result, I have provided the main website link for several online references instead of the direct (longtail) URL to the specific content. To access the exact reference, I encourage readers to visit the respective website and conduct a search using the website's navigation tools. I apologize for any inconvenience this may cause and appreciate your understanding.

Art by Mozelle Martin
(www.VisualDiversity.art)

Appendix

The following graphics serve as valuable support during challenging times. While it's important to note that not all monsters and creeps are narcissists, these sayings can offer assistance in coping with any difficulties you may encounter. Whenever you require an extra dose of inspiration, take a moment to read them and draw strength from their messages.

In the meantime, please follow these individuals on Twitter. Although I don't know any of them personally, they helped me get through this ordeal. Please tell them you saw their graphics in this book or tag them on the link.

https://twitter.com/Karma10120

https://twitter.com/Alissia94064624

https://twitter.com/Stopworkplacebu

https://twitter.com/unchainedin2021

https://twitter.com/Breakingfreetwo

https://twitter.com/PRINCESSLMNADE

https://twitter.com/NarcReco

https://twitter.com/Narcopath_UK

https://twitter.com/AwareOfTheNarc

https://twitter.com/Ryan_Daigler

https://twitter.com/narcissistfacts

https://twitter.com/LeavingNo

https://twitter.com/NarcissismFacts

NARCISSISTS ONLY TELL HALF THE STORY, THE HALF THAT MAKES THEM LOOK GOOD OR INNOCENT. THEY CONVENIENTLY LEAVE OUT THE OTHER HALF OF THE STORY. THE PART THAT SHOWS THEIR GUILT.
-MARIA CONSIGLIO

ABUSERS DON'T ABUSE EVERYONE. THEY ARE ACTUALLY VERY NICE TO SOME PEOPLE, POLITE AND HELPFUL. THATS WHY WHEN PROBLEMS ARISE, PEOPLE DO NOT BELIEVE THE VICTIM. THIS CAUSES THE VICTIM TO DOUBT THEMSELVES AND START TO INTERNALIZE THE ABUSE. THIS IS ANOTHER CRUEL FORM OF GAS LIGHTING. -MARIA CONSIGLIO

AND WHEN YOU FINALLY HEAL,
YOU WILL REALIZE THEY HAD
NOTHING TO OFFER YOU FROM
DAY ONE. JUST LIES AND
BULLSHIT.
IT WAS YOU WHO HAD
EVERYTHING THEY WANTED.
-UNKNOWN

NEVER TRY AND
DEFEND YOURSELF
AGAINST A NARCISSIST.
THEY ALREADY KNOW
YOU'RE RIGHT, THEY
JUST WANT YOU TO GO
CRAZY TRYING TO
PROVE IT.

Paper Quotes

A narcissist will hurt you and hurt you **again** and **again**, waiting for the moment that **you** retaliate.

Just so **they** can play the **victim**.

A WISE MAN SAID: DON'T SEEK REVENGE. THE ROTTEN FRUITS WILL FALL BY THEMSELVES.

THE NARCISSISTS SIDE
OF THE STORY WILL
ONLY INCLUDE YOUR
REACTION TO THEIR ABUSE

TOXIC PEOPLE
project their own
character defects onto
their victims. They do
this by accusing their
victim of the exact actions
they themselves do...
but deny.

When someone shows
you who they are believe
them; the first time.
MAYA ANGELOU

When a toxic person can no longer control you, they will try to control how others see you. This misinformation will feel unfair, but stay above it, trusting that other people will eventually see the truth - just like you did.

> **Narcissists seriously believe that it is abusive of *you* to object to them behaving abusively towards you.**
>
> **ANNIE KASZINA**

narcissists
create
storms but
blames
you when
it rains.

Believe in yourself,
work hard, and
don't let anyone
tell you what you
can or can't do.

@SeffSaid

Narcs are experts at making you feel you're wrong and they're right when in fact the opposite is true!

STAY AWAY FROM PEOPLE WHO ACT LIKE A VICTIM IN A PROBLEM THEY CREATED.

If you're going
to stalk me,
you could at
least like some
of my posts.

If I decided to block you it doesn't mean
I'm "petty" or "childish", it means I
decided to make my peace a priority.

You are toxic to my environment and I
will no longer grant you access to my
space.

I don't want to see your name, hear
your opinions or read your words and I
don't care what you're doing.

More Quotes to Empower Me:

Book Buddies Gift List: